An Important Message to Our Readers

This product provides information and general advice about the law. But laws and procedures change frequently, and they can be interpreted differently by different people. For specific advice geared to your specific situation, consult an expert. No book, software or other published material is a substitute for personalized advice from a knowledgeable lawyer licensed to practice law in your state.

9th edition

How to
Change
Your Name
in California

by Attorney Lisa Sedano

edited by Ralph Warner

NOLO

Keeping Up to Date

To keep its books up to date, Nolo issues new printings and new editions periodically. New printings reflect minor legal changes and technical corrections. New editions contain major legal changes, major text additions or major reorganizations. To find out if a later printing or edition of any Nolo book is available, call Nolo at 510-549-1976 or check our website: http://www.nolo.com.

To stay current, follow the "Update" service at our website: http://www.nolo.com. In another effort to help you use Nolo's latest materials, we offer a 35% discount off the purchase of the new edition of your Nolo book when you turn in the cover of an earlier edition. (See the "Special Upgrade Offer" in the back of the book.)

This book was last revised in: **NOVEMBER 2001.**

NINTH EDITION	November 2001
EDITOR	Ralph Warner
COVER DESIGN	Toni Ihara
BOOK DESIGN	Jaleh Doane
PRODUCTION	Sarah Hinman
PROOFREADING	Robert Wells
ILLUSTRATIONS	Mari Stein
INDEX	Patricia Deminna
PRINTING	Bertelsmann Services, Inc.

Sedano, Lisa, 1971-
    How to change your name in California / by Lisa Sedano. -- California 9th ed.
      p. cm.
    Rev. ed. of: How to change your name in California / by David Ventura Loeb & David W. Brown. -- California 8th ed. c1999.
    Includes index.
    ISBN 0-87337-598-X
    1. Names, Personal--Law and legislation--California.   I. Loeb, David V. How to change your name in California. II. Title.
    KFC109.L6 2000
    346.79401'2--dc21

00-39430

Quantity sales: For information on bulk purchases or corporate premium sales, please contact the Special Sales department. For academic sales or textbook adoptions, ask for Academic Sales, 800-955-4775. Nolo, 950 Parker St., Berkeley, CA, 94710.

Dedication

This book is dedicated to its original author, David Ventura Loeb. David died in September 1978 in the San Diego air disaster. At the time of his death, he was practicing law in Los Angeles, specializing in problems related to the entertainment field, and had just started another book for Nolo. Over the years, even as *How to Change Your Name* has been frequently rewritten to reflect changes in the law, we have continued to think of it as a living memorial to David and his love of life and his determination to help others. David was a good and kind man who left his friends and, hopefully, the readers of this book richer for knowing him.

Acknowledgements

Thanks to the many people who helped bring this book into being: Ken Twisselman, Suzanne Marychild, Ed Sherman, Trudy Ahlstrom, Mary-Lynne Fisher and David Loeb's friends: Nora, David and Darrell.

Special thanks to everyone whose time and expertise added to this book: Jake Warner, for his fine eye and tireless queries; Stephanie Harolde, for preparing copies of the manuscript; Terri Hearsh, for turning straw into gold in the production of this book and everyone else at Nolo whose hard work and enthusiasm add to every book.

Table of Contents

Introduction

1 The Different Ways to Change Your Name

 What's Your Name?

 Restrictions on New Names

Appendix

Index

Introduction

If you want to change your name but are reluctant—or unable—to pay several hundred dollars for an attorney, this book is for you. *How to Change Your Name in California* summarizes California law regarding name changes, and it provides all the forms and instructions you'll need to legally change your name in California.

Every year, thousands of people officially change their names. Following is a list of some common situations in which people seek a name change:

- **Name Changes After Marriage, Divorce or Annulment.** A woman may legally keep her birth name when she marries or she may adopt her husband's surname. Upon divorce or annulment, a woman may revert back to her birth or former name if she's been using her husband's name. A husband and wife can change their last names to a combination of the two or something altogether different. A divorced woman who has kept her "ex's" last name can easily change back to a former name (or a new name altogether) whenever she chooses.

- **Name Changes for Unmarried Couples.** A couple need not be legally married to assume the same last name. For example, some lesbian and gay couples choose to use the same last name as part of their commitment to one another. The name may be the last name of one of the members of the couple, a hyphenated combination of the names or an altogether different name.

- **Children's Names.** Often, a divorced parent with sole custody of the children wants to make sure the children have the same last name as the parent. If the custodial parent has changed her name since the marriage, she may want to change the children's names as well. Sometimes legal guardians prefer a child to have their last name. Other times, mature children have a preference for a certain name.

- **Immigrant Names.** Perhaps your great-grandfather Chassonovitch changed his name—or had his name changed for him—when he came to the United States in the 1880's. As Americans rediscover their heritages, they often want to change their last names back to their original ancestral names. Of course, there is also the reverse situation—for someone who feels no connection with a heavy six-syllable name, shortening the name or changing it altogether may be attractive.

- **Lifestyle and Convenience.** Why be called Rudolph, Marguerite or MaryAnn when you feel that Glenn, Jennifer or Penelope better expresses the real you? One Californian petitioned to change his name from Steamboat Robert E. Lee Green Leaf Strong Boy of the Wind to Robert Di Brezzio. Another who was tired of being last in every line changed his last name from Zywik to Aaron. You can be as creative as you want in selecting your name—few legal limitations exist on choice of name. (See Chapter 3, *Restrictions on New Names.*)

- **Religious and Political Names.** Some people may wish to change their names to reflect their religious or political beliefs. Famous political and religious leaders who have done this include Mother Teresa and Malcolm X. Some women feel that a birth name is an expression of a paternal heritage and decide to take on a form of their mother's name or a totally different name. For example, some women add the word "child" to their mother's first name and use this as a last name—such as Suzanne Marychild.

How to Change Your Name in California provides help for all of these situations. The steps are the same no matter what new name you choose. Whether you have a common or uncommon reason for wanting to change your name—and whether you want to use a common or uncommon name—this book will help you accomplish your goal. It's easy.

To make it easy for you to use this book, we've used the following icons to point you to important or relevant information:

 This alerts you to a practical tip or good idea.

 This is a caution to slow down and consider potential problems.

 This icon means that you may be able to skip some material that doesn't apply to your situation.

 This icon lets you know where you can read more about the particular issue or topic discussed in the text; or refers you to related information in another chapter of this book.

This icon tells you that the form being discussed in the text can be found as a tear-out in the Appendix.

■

The Different Ways to Change Your Name

California offers its residents several relatively simple and easy ways to change their names. This chapter gives you an overview of the different methods, so you can determine which one is right for you.

No matter what method you use, after you officially change your name in California your new name will be valid everywhere. That's because the U.S. Constitution guarantees that the legal procedures of one state must be recognized by all.

A. How to Change an Adult's Name

In California, adults have always had the right to use the first, middle and last names of their choice. In fact, California adults have the legal right to change their names simply by using their desired new names. You don't have to go to court and you don't have to file any forms or pay any fees. This method for changing your name is called the "Usage" method.

If it's that easy, why would anyone go to court to change her name? Because, although you have the legal right to change your name without filing court papers, as a practical matter it can be difficult to get state and federal agencies to accept your new name without official authentication. For this reason, it is often better to change your name by going to court where you will receive a court order that serves as proof of your new name.

The available methods for changing an adult's name are:
- Usage (simply using a new name)
- Court Petition (filing a name change petition in court), and
- Other Court Order (obtaining a name change as part of another court proceeding, such as a divorce).

1. Usage Method

California judges have consistently affirmed an adult's traditional (common law) right to change her name change without going to court. (For a list of court opinions affirming this right, see Chapter 8.) Under California law, court procedures for name changes were created only to provide official recognition of a person's name change, not as a substitute for changing it by Usage. In short, you don't *have* to go to court to change your name; you only need to go to court if you want the state's official stamp of approval. But as we'll explain, as the world gets ever more bureaucratic and pressure increases to stop unscrupulous people from stealing another person's name (identity theft), getting this stamp of approval has become more and more convenient and in some cases necessary for getting your new name accepted.

Just a few years ago, this book wholeheartedly recommended the Usage method. No question, it's potentially a great way to change your name because it involves nothing more complicated than consistently using your new name. As long as you use the name in all aspects of your life (professional, social, etc.), you have legally changed your name. Pretty easy.

But today there is a strong trend to require official proof of name changes. Governmental regulations, created to combat modern types of fraud such as identity theft, are quickly making it more difficult to have a new name accepted without official documentation. No longer can you just walk into many government offices, tell the clerk you've changed your name and have your name changed in the records. And even where it is still possible to get a Usage method name change accepted, doing so can be as much trouble as simply going to court and getting a judge's official okay. The trend towards making name changes more complicated is exemplified by regulations adopted by the Department of Motor Vehicles ("DMV"), which make it difficult to change your name without a court order. Obviously, driver's licenses and ID cards issued by the DMV are two of the most essential pieces of identification in our country. Without the ability to list your new name on one of these, your name change will be seriously incomplete.

Although it is getting harder to have your Usage name change accepted, if you're willing to give it time and effort, often it can still be done. If you are determined to try this approach, the best way to start is by having your name changed in records and on IDs from agencies which aren't yet requiring official proof of a name change. For example, even without a court order, you may be able to have the DMV change your name if you start with another type of government documentation first, such as a Social Security card or a passport. These agencies currently don't require official proof of a name change. If you are able to demonstrate to these agencies that you really are using the name, you should be able to get identification in the new name. You should then be able to take the new ID to the DMV and use it to obtain a DMV card in your new name. We describe this process in Chapter 7, How to Get Your New Name Accepted.

Although today the Usage method is far harder to pull off than it used to be, a few people still prefer it because it is a more private process. Going to court to change your name will create a public court record and will require you to publish a notice of your name change in a local newspaper. Therefore, if you have personal reasons for keeping your name change private, you may shrink from the Court Petition process. But, while it's part of the public record, a court name change isn't all that "public"—for example, it will only be published in the fine print of the legal notices, which few people read.

⚠ The Usage method is unavailable to inmates, parolees and registered sex offenders. Under California Code of Civil Procedure § 1279.5(a), state prison inmates, persons on parole and those required to register as sex offenders cannot legally change their names by the Usage method. If this is your situation, you can change your name only by going to court. See Chapter 6, Court Petition, for more information; and go to

Nolo's website at http://www.nolo.com to read the statute in full. On Nolo's home page under the Free Legal Information and Tools, you'll see a link to Nolo's Legal Research Center, where you'll find a link to California's statutes.

2. Going to Court

Petitioning the Superior Court to officially grant a change of name is now the most widely accepted way to accomplish this task. It involves filing several forms with the court and shepherding them through the court's name change process. The result is a court order (decree), recognizing your new name. Fortunately, the forms you'll need to fill out are straightforward and the court procedures are streamlined. This book will walk you through the process, step-by-step. Unless you qualify to include a name change in another court proceeding, such as a divorce or an adoption, we recommend the Court Petition as the best way to change your name.

Under the Court Petition method, you will ask your local court to issue a decree officially changing your name. This is a common and simple procedure. California law requires judges to issue adult name change decrees upon request, unless there is an important reason not to. Therefore, the law is very strongly on your side. Unless someone objects to your name change, it is likely the court will issue your name change decree without a hearing. (See Chapter 3, Restrictions on New Names.)

To use the Court Petition method, read this book and follow its instructions to complete the required court forms. There is usually no need to write up your own paperwork—you simply use pre-printed forms issued by the State of California and contained in this book. In the few relatively rare instances where additional forms are needed, we show you how to create them.

Court filing fees for a name change petition are around $200. The court may waive your fees if you have a low income (follow our instructions to prepare and submit the necessary paperwork). If you hire an attorney, you could expect to spend upwards of $500 or more to complete the procedure. By following the instructions in this book, you can easily and successfully do the job yourself. (See Chapter 6, Court Petition, for detailed information on this process.) Or, if preparing the necessary forms is too much of a hassle, you may want to hire a reasonably inexpensive nonlawyer legal document preparation service to help with the paperwork (see Chapter 8, Section C, for more on how this works).

After your papers are filled out and filed with the court, you will be required to publish a short notice in a newspaper stating that you are changing your name. The newspaper will normally charge a fee of between $40 and $200, depending on your area and the newspaper you choose. Once you've done this, the process is nearly complete. Unless someone objects to your name change (this is very rare), the court will likely approve your petition without your need to attend a court hearing. Occasionally, a brief appearance before a judge is required. If so, you can easily handle the procedure on your own following the instructions in this book.

Filing and guiding your petition through court will take a bit of time and effort. However, the Court Petition process is not as daunting as it may seem, and you'll be pleased with the results.

You may actually prefer a court-ordered name change. Like becoming a U.S. citizen, getting a divorce or participating in other important legal procedures, many people want their name change to be included in an official court order which is part of the public record. And this is true even though it's just as legal to change your name following the Usage method.

There may be a third avenue available to you for changing your name. Although it still involves accomplishing a court-ordered name change, a woman (or man) obtaining a divorce or annulment in California can simply ask the judge who handles her divorce to officially restore her birth or former

name in the court's decree. By California law, the judge must do so upon the woman's request, even if she did not include the request in the original divorce or annulment petition. (Cal. Fam. Code §§ 2080, 2081.) A woman (or man) who is divorced in California and who did not change her name during that proceeding can later ask the divorce court to restore her birth or former name at any time after the divorce becomes final. All you have to do is file a one-page form with the court that divorced you. If you are divorcing or were divorced in California and want to return to a former name, we strongly recommend this procedure, which is cheaper and more convenient than other available methods. (See Chapter 4, Marriage, Divorce and Custody.)

B. How to Change a Child's Name

Where both parents agree, changing a child's name can often be as easy as changing an adult's name. However, if the parents are at odds over whether to change a child's name, it can be difficult or even impossible. There are three possible ways to change a child's name. These are:

- **Court Petition.** Petitioning a court is the most common method for changing a child's name. This process, which is fully explained in this book, is much the same as for an adult applicant, unless one parent objects, in which case a contested court fight may occur.
- **Adoption.** Changing a child's name during an adoption or other court procedure works well, but is only available if you happen to be participating in the related proceeding.
- **Birth Certificate.** Unfortunately, a birth certificate can only be changed in very limited circumstances, as discussed in detail in Chapter 5.

The Usage method doesn't work for minors. A minor can't legally change his or her name simply by using a new one.

1. A Court Petition to Change a Child's Name

Both parents or one parent alone can file a name change petition on behalf of a child. Where both parents request the change, courts normally grant the request automatically. A child's court-appointed legal guardian (a grandparent, for example) can also file the petition. If the child has no court-appointed guardian, an adult relative or close friend can file the petition. Chapter 6, Court Petition, describes the court process in detail (for adults and children) and also contains a section on changing a child's name.

When one parent alone petitions to change a child's name, state law requires that the other parent be given advance notice of the proposed name change. The court will require the petitioning parent to "serve" the court papers on the other parent or provide an explanation of why this is not possible. (This is covered in detail in Chapter 6, Court Petition, Section C.) If the other parent doesn't respond or agrees to the name change in writing, chances are good the court will approve it.

If the other parent objects to the child's name change, the court will grant the petition only if it is "in the best interests of the child" (Cal. Civ. Proc. Code § 1278.5). In order to determine which name is in the child's best interests, the court will hold a hearing, so each parent can state his or her arguments and, if the child is old enough, the court may choose to interview the child. (For more on the "best interests" standard, see Chapter 6, Section A.)

2. Change a Child's Name As Part of an Adoption

As with an adult, a court can include a child's name change in another ongoing proceeding. For example, adopting parents almost always request their adopted child's name be changed as part of the adoption order. If for some reason the court fails to change an adopted child's name, the adoptive parents may file a petition on their adopted child's behalf. In this case, the parents will use the general Court Petition process, and they can follow the instructions in Chapter 6, Court Petition.

3. Birth Certificate

In certain very limited circumstances, including typographic errors and incomplete parental information, a child's birth certificate can be changed or amended to reflect a different name. If you are able to change a child's name on his birth certificate, his name is officially changed and you don't need to go to court. Chapter 5, Birth Certificates, describes the circumstances in which the state will allow a new birth certificate to be issued or an existing certificate to be amended. ■

CHAPTER

2

What's Your Name?

A. What's Your Name?

Your name is what you go by, right? Maybe. For people who have used a number of names over the years—or are halfway through the process of adopting a new name—being able to state their own name isn't so simple. In fact, their first job in the name change process is to determine what their current legal name really is.

➡ **Skip ahead if you have only used one name.** This chapter helps people who have used a number of names to sort out questions regarding multiple names. If you have only used one name in your life—or are using this book to change a child's name—skip ahead to Chapter 3.

For people who have used a number of names, the following questions may arise:

- What if you've already been using your "new" name? Does that mean it's already your official name?
- What if you have more than one name? Between misspellings, nicknames, a marriage and a divorce, you may have collected a string of names, with different ones appearing on different documents and IDs. How do you sort out which is your present name?
- What if you use several first names (you were born Elizabeth, used to be called Liz and are now Lisa) and want to change all of your documents to, say, Lisa?

There are two reasons why it's important to try to work through these and other perplexing name situations to legally determine what your official name is. First, the answer will tell you whether you need to go to court to have your name officially changed. For example, if you've been using your new name exclusively for years and especially if it appears on your driver's license, you may not need to petition a court to change your name—your new name may already be your legal name. Second, assuming you do go to court, you'll need to know how to list yourself on your court documents. The process of thinking through your current name situation will help you get a handle on all the names you've ever used and what name you will use as your present name on your court documents.

Start by making a list of all the names you currently use and what important documents each appears on. To jog your memory of every place you need to check to see how your name is listed, check out Chapter 7 where we list the most important governmental agencies and private businesses that keep track of names.

B. Multiple Last Names

If you have used one last name consistently for the last couple of years and it appears on most of your paperwork, including your driver's license, Social Security card and other key documents, you won't need to go to court to adopt it. Even if this name is different from your birth name, it's now your legal name.

EXAMPLE: When Joanne Brown was married, she took her husband's name and became Joanne Landon. Ten years later, they divorced. She decided to keep her married name. After a few years, however, she no longer wanted her husband's name. But she didn't want to "take a step back" and return to her own family name, either. Instead, Joanne coined a new name for herself—Brandon—and had all of her records changed to this name. Five years later, she worries that Brandon isn't her "official" name. Does she need to go to court? No, since she has used her new name consistently and had all her records changed, her name change is complete under the Usage method. (See Chapter 1, Section A.)

Joanne was able to completely accomplish her name change without going to court, but many people these days are not so lucky. If you have used your new name for less than five years, and/or if you have not been able to get all your records changed to your new name, you may need to go to court. As we discussed in Chapter 1, it's tougher now to avoid going to court and change your name via the Usage method.

If you have used a number of last names over the years and your records reflect this confusion, you may need to go to court to straighten out your name situation. This is particularly likely to be true if, try as you might, you aren't sure what your current legal name is. Consider the following example.

EXAMPLE: Sidney Lakes had a terrible relationship with her father growing up and, at the age of 16, started going by her mother's family name, Becker. When Sidney Becker got married, she became Sidney Loudon. A few years later she divorced and remarried, becoming Sidney Li. Sidney has always hated dealing with bureaucracies, so never bothered to inform many of them of her frequent name changes. As a result, her wallet is filled with cards in four different names and her filing cabinet where she keeps important documents reflects the same confusion. Sidney, who has now been Mrs. Sidney Li for five years and plans to keep that name until death do us part, is ready to clean up the mess. What is Sidney's official name? If it isn't Li, does she need to go to court to make it clear that it will be?

It's not clear what Sidney's official name is—in fact, she may have more than one official name. For this reason, her simpler course of action is to go to court to straighten out her confused name situation. True, Sidney might be able to get all her records changed to Li without going to court, but there are two important reasons why this is not her best approach. First, a court order will clarify her name situation quickly and easily. Second, since Sidney hates dealing with bureaucracies, she'll dread the involved process of trying to get agencies and businesses to informally change all their records. By comparison, going to court will be painless.

Occasionally, the government is to blame for multiple names. Today this most often happens because a government official makes a mistake. In the past, it also frequently occurred when an immigration official or someone dealing with Native Americans arbitrarily changed a name to something more "American."

EXAMPLE: Deer Walking On Frozen Lake was born in Oklahoma in 1962. His birth certificate lists his full name. When his parents signed up for his Social Security card, however, the bureaucrat helping them with their paperwork thought he should put the name into a more American form: Deer Frozen-Lake. When Deer was old enough to get his driver's license, the DMV listed his name on his license as Deer W. Lake. Deer now wants to get all his paperwork in one name—and for simplicity, he has decided he wants it to be Deer Walking. What is Deer's official name and should he go to court?

At this point, Deer may not have just one legal name. But, because his birth certificate contains all the variations of the name he wants to use in the future, he may be able to get all his records changed to Deer Walking by just showing his birth certificate. If he runs into trouble, he should go to court.

In a situation like Sidney's or Deer's, it may be difficult to figure out what your one real name is. Your best approach is to go through all your paperwork to see if one name appears on most of your key government-issued documents, such as your driver's license, Social Security card and passport. If one name sticks out, it is probably your official name. You may be able to change your name on other documents following the Usage method. But if a couple of names share the spotlight, chances are you'll need to go to court to settle on one.

Assuming you do go to court to straighten out your personal name mess, what name do you list on your court documents as your "present" (official current) name? You should normally list either the name that is on your birth certificate or, if that name isn't on other documents you currently use (the deed to your house, your bank accounts and your driver's license, for example), you should use the name that is on the most government IDs and records. In addition, you should also list all the other names you use or have recently used as AKAs (also known as). Do this even if the name you most want to change is one of these AKAs.

> **EXAMPLE:** Gina's birth certificate says Gina Lopez, as do her Social Security card and driver's license. She took her husband's name when she married, becoming Gina St. Clair, but never got around to changing her name on these important government documents. On new documents, though, she used her married name. These included the deed to her house, her credit cards and insurance cards. Gina divorced and kept the name St. Clair. By this point, she had used the name St. Clair for ten years, and it was on all her business and personal documents. A few years later, she decides to change her name to something new: Gina Lorraine. What is Gina's official present name and how should she list her name on her government documents?
>
> Even though St. Clair is on more documents than Lopez, and even though Gina probably thinks of her present name as St. Clair, her official name is probably Lopez. That's because it is on her most important pieces of identification: her birth certificate, Social Security card and driver's license. When Gina goes to court to change her last name to Lorraine, she should list her name as: "Gina Lopez a.k.a. Gina St. Clair."

Don't worry if this AKA business seems confusing now. We'll go over it again in Chapter 6, Court Petition, as we help you fill out the court forms line by line.

C. Multiple First Names

A different situation is presented when you want to change your first name but not your last name. Government offices are generally more flexible when it comes to changing a first name. In many circumstances, you'll find that they will change your first name in their records without a court order. This is especially likely if you can show you've been using the new name. The same holds true for nicknames as well.

> **EXAMPLE:** Her birth certificate says "Melissa Price," but since she was a babe in arms everyone has called her Marley. Marley calls herself by this name and even got it accepted on her school documents and her driver's license. But when her parents applied for her passport, they remembered what it said on her birth certificate and listed her as Melissa. When Marley graduated from college, she decided she should use a more "mature" name. Because she liked the name Melinda more than Melissa, she asked her friends to call her that. But old habits die hard, and she still signs her name Marley half the time. Does Melissa/Marley/Melinda need to go to court to resolve the three-name confusion?
>
> Before we can answer that question, Marley must decide what she wants her "official" name to be. Whether it's Marley, Melinda or even good old Melissa, she should start being consistent in how she lists herself on records and IDs. After she makes her decision, she should work on getting all her records changed to her one official name. Especially if she uses Melissa, she can do this without a court order because she has her birth certificate to back her up. Marley, too, should be no problem, since she has so many documents in that name. Getting Melinda accepted by the Usage method will be tougher since it's an entirely new name. But again, since changing a first name is far less problematic than tinkering with a last name, she may eventually succeed. If she wants to make her name Melissa quickly and easily, she may find that it's

less trouble to go to court and make the change. (See Chapter 1, The Different Ways to Change Your Name.)

Using a nickname is no problem. One choice that Melissa/Marley/Melinda (and everyone else) has is to use one name for all business purposes and another for social interactions. For example, Walter can stick to his rather serious moniker for official purposes but still ask everyone he meets socially to call him Joe. It's perfectly legal.

D. Pen, Stage and Other Business Names

You might be confused as to what your one official name is if you have used a pen name, stage name or other business name for many years and have gradually begun to also use it in your personal life. These are names people have taken on for purely business purposes. For example, if a jockey named Sebastian Monkevitcz rides under the sobriquet Johnny Monk, Monkevitcz is still his name as long as he has kept it on all his personal records. Or put another way, pen names or other names used for business purposes do not become your official name unless you have started to use the name exclusively. This is true because, as we mentioned in Chapter 1, a name change by Usage is accomplished only if you use your new name in all, or at least most, aspects of your life.

Therefore, if you simply want to make sure that your business name is not your official name, you won't need to go to court—so long as the name you want as your official name is the name that you currently have on your significant records. But if you want your pen name to be your official name, going to court is a good idea. Sebastian Monkevitcz can try to make the change without a court decree—for instance, by showing government offices all the programs, newspaper articles and business contracts that mention refer to him as Johnny Monk—but he'll probably find it far simpler to have a judge issue a decree (court order) acknowledging the change.

If you decide to go to court—because you want to change your name to your pen name or to an entirely different name—be sure to list your official present name on your court documents. Again, your official name is the one that is currently on all your records and government documents—not your pen name. ■

Restrictions on New Names

One court has defined a person's name as "the distinctive characterization in words by which he is known and distinguished from others." (*Putnam v. Bessom*, 291 Mass. 217 (1935).) Leaving aside the question of why judges can't learn to speak English, most names which people select as their "distinctive characterizations"—or, more likely, which their parents pick for them—are acceptable under the law. Put more directly, there are very few legal limits on the name you may choose.

If you seek to change your name by Court Petition, the judge can refuse to grant your new name only if a substantial reason exists for the denial. Under California law, "substantial reasons" include the following:

- You may not choose a name for "fraudulent purposes" (meaning, you intend to do something illegal using the name). For example, you may not legally change your name if your reason is to avoid paying debts, to hide from people trying to sue you or to get away with a crime.
- You may not "interfere with the rights of others," which generally means choosing the name of a famous person with the intent to somehow profit from doing so.
- You may not use a name that would be "intentionally confusing." This might be choosing a number or type of punctuation for your name (for example, "10" or "?").
- You may not choose a name that could be considered "fighting words," which includes threatening or obscene words, racial slurs or other words likely to incite violence.

Unless the judge is aware of a substantial reason to deny your application, such as the ones mentioned above, she has a duty to approve your name change.

A. Famous Names

Famous people, such as celebrities, politicians and other public figures, do not have exclusive rights to their names. For example, if you look in the telephone book of a large city, you're likely to find a listing for George Bush, Michael Jordan or Michael Jackson.

It follows that you can normally adopt the name of a famous person as long as:

- you're not adopting the name with fraudulent purposes
- you're not likely to be confused with the famous person (which could happen if you live nearby or have a similar profession)
- you will not benefit commercially or economically by using the name, and
- your use of the name will not cast the famous person in a negative light.

Some years ago, an aspiring actor with an exceptional talent for impersonating the movie star Peter Lorre petitioned the court to have his name changed to Peter Lorre. The court refused the petition when the real Peter Lorre objected to the name change. (*In re Weingand*, 231 Cal. App. 2d 289, 41 Cal. Rptr. 778 (1964).) In another case, a California resident petitioned a Los Angeles court to change his name to Jesus Christ. The court clerk made a diligent attempt to determine if the name change was fraudulent. He found a Jesus Witness Christ living in East Los Angeles and a Jesus J. Christ in Santa Monica. It turns out that Christ is a German last name and Jesus is a common Hispanic name. The court found no proof of fraud and approved the name change petition.

Avoid famous names if possible. Although it's true that you can choose any name, no matter how famous, as long as you don't intend to misuse the name in any of the ways discussed, it's also true that choosing a very well-known name is likely to red flag your petition and cause a judge to question you closely. So if you want to change your last name to Greenspan, things will surely go easier if you choose Fred, rather than Alan, for your first name.

Famous Names and the Right of Publicity

The right of publicity makes it unlawful to use another's "persona" for economic gain. For example, if you use the name or image of a famous person to advertise your product without his or her consent, that person can sue you for hefty damages, since he, not you, has the right to profit from publicizing his name. In California, this right of publicity extends to the names of famous people who have died. Their heirs have a legal right to prevent you from using the name for purposes of economic gain for years after the death of their family member (Cal. Civ. Code § 990). Therefore, if you take on the name of a famous person, either alive or dead, you could face a lawsuit if you use the name for economic gain. Only a handful of other states have similar laws. Case law concerning these matters is frequently contradictory.

B. Fictitious Names

Fictitious names, such as the names of characters (Harry Potter) or companies (IBM), are almost always protected by a combination of copyright, trademark or corporate law. If you plan to use such a name to make money or promote yourself or a product, you run the risk of a legal battle. You could protect yourself by getting advance consent from the person or company with rights to the name, but this is something that rights-holders will rarely give without a fat fee. In theory, you are allowed to use someone else's fictitious name as your personal name as long as you have no intent to commercialize or publicize the name (after all, lots of people are named Potter). But here again, it makes sense to modify the desired name so it is similar but not identical to the well-known fictitious name. For example, call yourself Daniel Potter or perhaps even Harold Potter, but not Harry Potter. Doing this avoids the possibility of a court fight over your intent.

C. Initials, Numbers and One-Word Names

An initial is legally sufficient as a first, middle or last name. The initial does not have to stand for a longer name. Well-known examples are Malcolm X and Harry S Truman. The "S'" for the former President's middle name never stood for anything—the letter itself was his middle name.

A court may use its discretion in allowing a petitioner to adopt a number as a name. For example, a man named Thomas Ritchie III failed in his court petition to change his entire name to the Roman numeral "III." The court determined that a Roman numeral is simply not a name and was inherently confusing. (*In re Ritchie*, 159 Cal. App. 3d 1070, 206 Cal. Rptr. 239 (1984).) Minnesota's Supreme Court ruled that a man who wanted to change his name to the number "1069" could not legally do so, but suggested that "Ten Sixty-Nine" might be acceptable. (*Application of Dengler*, 287 N.W.2d 637 (1979).)

California statutory law does not specifically authorize you to change your name to just one word (like "Monkey-man" or "Freedom"). But in an age where Social Security numbers and other numerical identifiers are increasingly used by governments, banks and other important bureaucracies, and the main purpose of a name is to identify you to friends, family and business associates, one name should be as good as two or three. And for many purposes it already is. California judges have approved one-word names on numerous occasions. The State Registrar of Vital Statistics accepts birth certificates which list only a last name for the baby. A contract signed in just one name is considered valid. The Registrar of Voters reports that they have registered people who changed their names by Court Petition to just one name ("especially rock stars").

Many other states agree that if you want your only moniker to be Moniker, that's okay. For example, in the Missouri case of *In re Reed*, 584 S.W.2d 103 (1979), an appeals court allowed a petitioner to change his name to "Sunshine."

Adding just one initial makes a one-word name work. Practically, you will run into hassles if you only use one name. Every form you fill out requests at least two names, and many computers have trouble fathoming single names. You'll also likely run into resistance from at least some bureaucrats who think having just one name is not acceptable. But if you try using one name and find that it's too much trouble, you can make even the fussiest computer happy by adopting a single initial for your first or last name. For example, just plain George could become O. George or George O.

D. Racial Slurs, Fighting Words and Other Forbidden Names

You may not use the Court Petition method to adopt a name that includes a racial slur or other words that offend others so intensely that they are likely to respond with violence. An African-American educator from Thousand Oaks, California, attempted to change his name to "Misteri Nigger" (pronounced "Mr. Nigger"). By using this name, he hoped "to steal the stinging degradation—the thunder—from the word nigger," and thus, "to conquer racial hatred." Nevertheless, the court ruled that a racial epithet—that is, a disparaging or abusive word that may be a "fighting word"—may not be adopted by the Court Petition method. (*Lee v. Ventura County Superior Court*, 9 Cal. App. 4th 510, 11 Cal. Rptr. 2d 763 (1992).) So, regardless of your

intentions in choosing a new name, a court may deny it if it is an ethnic or racial slur or includes words of threat or profanity.

But can you change your name to something like Pregnant Chad or Merri Christmas? That depends on the particular judge, who has discretion in deciding whether to grant a name change. In theory, both of these should be fine since they aren't profane and don't constitute an ethnic or racial slur. Of the two, Pregnant Chad is more problematic because some judge with no sense of humor and a long memory might say it amounts to fighting words. But what about Merri Christmas? At least one judge has already approved it.

Of course, you can always appeal the judge's decision. This process involves taking your case to the California Court of Appeal. Doing this will be time-consuming and, if you hire a lawyer, expensive. Because it is almost never done, we do not cover the appeals procedure in this book.

Restricted Names and the Usage Method

If you hope to take on a name that for one reason or another a court is unlikely to grant, you might think: "Why bother with going to court—it will be easier to just use my new name." After all, California's common law allows people to change their names by the Usage method. By choosing this approach you could avoid a judge (as well as anyone who wants to formally object to your name). Subject to the normal problems inherent in changing a name via the Usage method (see Chapter 1, Section A), this might work if the name isn't too awful. But if you try to establish your name as Bad Ass Brown or Mother Phucker, you're sure to have problems getting the new name accepted. And in situations where you are ripping off a famous person's name and using it in an attempt to profit or invade her privacy, the fact that you made the change by Usage and not going to court won't protect you from a lawsuit.

E. Titles and Forms of Address

A title or form of address, such as Mr. or Ms., is not considered part of a legal name. You are allowed to use whatever title or form of address you like, regardless of age or marital status. You are also free *not* to use any title, if you don't want to. For example, a married woman is free to use Miss, Ms., no title at all or the more traditional Mrs.

Only one limit exists in using titles: You cannot use a particular title in an attempt to commit fraud, such as to appear married when you are not. The same holds true for professional titles, such as Dr., M.D., Esq. or J.D. You cannot use any of these titles in a way that implies you are a licensed physician or attorney.

A judge might deny your name change request if you wanted to change your first name to a title. For example, the name Mrs. Smith might be considered inherently confusing, especially if a man wanted to use this name. A court might allow a name such as Doctor Jones, but not if it found the public would be confused into believing the person was actually a doctor.

F. Names You May Give a Child at Birth

In this country, it is common for children to take their father's last name. This is a customary practice; it is not required by law. Customs vary in other countries. In many Spanish-speaking countries, a child's last name is a combination of the mother's and father's last names. In medieval France, it was common practice for girls to take their mother's last name and boys to take their father's last name.

In California, you can legally give your children any last name you wish, so long as it does not violate any of the restrictions described in this chapter. For example, parents could give their child:

- the mother's last name
- the father's last name
- a combination of both last names (for example, Duffey-Loeb), or
- a last name that is totally unrelated to either of the parents. For example, several decades ago the actress Jane Fonda and her political activist husband, Tom Hayden, named their son Troy O'Donovan Garity.

Children's Names and Paternity

Giving a child a certain man's last name does not make the man the legal father of the child, nor does it make him legally responsible for the child. Paternity (the legal recognition of fatherhood) and names are two completely different legal animals. Nevertheless, it is always a mistake to give a child the last name of a man who is not the true father because you hope it will get him to assume parental and financial responsibility. It will not make him legally responsible for the child unless he currently is your husband, and later you will have a hard time getting the name changed on the birth certificate.

When you have a child, a hospital worker or the person who delivered the baby is legally required to complete the birth certificate with information that you give them and then file it with the state. Before you sign the completed birth certificate, make sure the child has the name you've chosen and that all the information is correct. As we describe in Chapter 5, birth certificates are very hard to change.

Marriage, Divorce and Custody

Marriage and divorce are the two most common reasons why adults change their names. In both cases, the main rule is simple: Whether you change your name is entirely up to you. A woman who marries may adopt her husband's last name, keep her birth name or even create a new name. The same goes for men. Today it's not as unusual as it once was for newly married men to change their names to reflect their new union rather than continue to use their family name.

At divorce, the same options exist: A spouse has the choice of keeping a married name or returning to a birth or former name. Over time, women (or men) may change their names a number of times. For example, a woman might take her husband's last name when she marries, resume her birth name when she divorces and change to her new husband's last name when she remarries.

"Birth name" = "maiden name."
Traditionally, the family name a woman was born into was referred to as her "maiden name." But way back in 1974, the California legislature changed maiden name to "birth name" in many of the more important laws dealing with names. For this reason, the term birth name is used in this book, and when dealing with the legal system, should be preferred to maiden name. In situations where a divorcing person wants to reassume the name of a previous spouse, the term "former name" is most appropriate.

A. Marriage

People who marry are free to keep their own names, adopt one spouse's last name for use by both, hyphenate their names or choose a completely new name. In many Western countries, women have traditionally taken their husband's family name. Women are free to keep their own family names, though, and many women do. Other naming options exist for married couples. For ex-

ample, a couple could adopt a hyphenated combination of their last names (Him-Her or Her-Him) or pick an altogether different last name.

1. Keeping Your Name When You Marry

Women used to ask whether they were required to adopt their husband's last name when they married. Nowadays, most people don't need to ask. There is no law in California that requires a woman to assume her husband's name upon marriage—and today many choose not to.

By law, a woman cannot be discriminated against in businesses or credit matters because of her name. California law requires that all businesses accept a married woman's birth or former name if she regularly uses it, regardless of her marital status (Cal. Civ. Proc. Code §1279.6). The law also requires credit card companies to issue credit cards in the name a woman requests, be it her birth name or married name. However, the credit card company is allowed to insist that a married woman establish an account separate from her husband's (Cal. Civ. Code § 1747.81).

Look Up the Law

How to look up the law. All California laws can be read free of charge at http://www.nolo.com. From the Free Information and Tools section of Nolo's home page, just click through on the State Laws section of Nolo's Legal Research Center.

If you want to keep your name when you marry, simply don't change it. There's no need to file any documents with the court, since a married woman acquires her husband's name only if she chooses to. Just don't use your husband's name and keep your own name on all records.

It makes little sense to notify agencies and businesses you deal with that you got married but don't want your records changed. You will only risk confusing people. It's possible that some of your records may get changed to your husband's name when the news of your marriage filters through the bureaucracy. If so, you will have to contact someone about changing those records back.

It's not uncommon for women who are or have been married to use more than one name. For example, a newly married woman may change some of her records to her new married name while leaving others in her birth name. Women who don't consistently use the same name are bound to run into occasional confusion and inconvenience. For example, a woman with a bank account in her birth name may run into trouble if she tries to cash checks with an ID showing her married name. She'll probably need to supply a copy of her marriage license or a piece of convincing ID that still shows her birth name.

A Historical Note: "Lucy Stoners"

Over the years, many married women have retained their birth names. Pioneering American Suffragette Lucy Stone began the tradition in 1855, when she created a furor as the first American woman to keep her name after marriage. In Stone's honor, Ruth Hale, a New York journalist, founded the Lucy Stone League in 1921. A "Lucy Stoner" is now defined in many dictionaries as "a person who advocates the keeping of their own names by married women." Some of the early Lucy Stoners included Amelia Earhart, Edna St. Vincent Millay and Margaret Mead.

2. Changing Your Name When You Marry

Until recently, it was customary in our society for a woman to adopt her husband's last name when she married. Though the custom may be eroding, or at least losing it's pervasiveness, it is still very common for women to take their husband's names. People (even bureaucrats!) usually accept the new name without a hassle because the practice is so widely followed. Sometimes they'll even throw in a smile and a "congratulations." Because this type of name change is so accepted, it is one of the few types of name changes for which we still unreservedly recommend the Usage method.

Under the DMV's name change regulations, an applicant can use a marriage certificate to prove a name change. Therefore, there is no need to go to court to have your driver's license or ID card reflect your spouse's last name. And with your new name on your driver's license or ID card, you'll have no problem getting your name changed elsewhere. If you don't have one of these cards or if you want to get started before your new card comes in the mail, you should be able to have other records changed either by showing businesses and agencies a copy of your marriage certificate or just telling them you got married.

3. Returning to Birth or Former Name While Married

Over time, the name you use after marriage will appear in more and more records—your driver's license, tax returns and credit cards. You can save yourself considerable angst later by making sure you are happy using your spouse's name *before* you have any records changed. After making the change, a surprising number of women wish they had instead kept their birth name. But after years of usage, many conclude it's too much trouble to re-adopt their birth name.

California courts have upheld the right of women to retain or return to their birth or a former name. Lower courts routinely grant married women's petitions to return to their birth names. In analogous court cases, it has been held that a married woman may be sued in her birth name, and a wife's last name does not automatically change when her husband changes his name, unless she consents. (*Sousa v. Freitas*, 10 Cal. App. 3d 660, 89 Cal. Rptr. 485 (1970).)

If you go to court to change your name to a name other than your husband's, on rare occasions a male judge may ask whether your husband agrees with the change. The law does not require your husband to co-sign the petition or attend the hearing (in the unusual case that the court holds a hearing). But, your husband is free to do so and for personal reasons you may want him to. But if it is important to you to make the change on your own (even over the objections of your spouse), there is nothing in the law to stop you.

If you return to your birth (or a former) name, be prepared to deal with the fact that some agencies or credit granters may falsely conclude you have divorced. As part of the process of notifying them of your new (old) name, you'll want to make it clear that no divorce is involved.

B. Divorce and Annulment

Women facing a divorce or annulment have the same number of options for their name as they did when they got married. If they have taken their husband's last name, divorcing women are entitled to keep that name. They can also return to a birth name or to a former name from a previous marriage. Each woman facing divorce can make this choice for herself. If she has children from the marriage, her ability to keep or change her name isn't affected by who has custody or what last name the children have. Because the same rules govern divorce and annulment, for the sake of brevity we refer only to divorce throughout the rest of this section.

If a woman decides to keep her husband's name, she can continue to go by the first and last name of her ex-husband—for example, Mrs. Robert Smith—if she chooses to. The only exception to this rule is that a divorced woman may not use her married name fraudulently. For example, she cannot use the name in order to falsely pass herself off as still married to her ex-husband or to avoid creditors.

Many women who are divorcing choose to change their names. Often, they want to return to their birth name or to a name from a previous marriage. California law has created an easy way for women (and men) who are divorcing (or who have divorced in California), to officially return to a former name. You can use this procedure if you are in the midst of a divorce, or you can use it after the divorce is final.

1. Returning to Your Former Name—During the Divorce Proceeding

If you are divorcing (or having your marriage annulled) in California, the Family Code makes it easy for you to return to your birth name or a former name. At any time during the divorce proceeding, you can ask the court to restore your name. Under Family Code sections 2080 and 2081, the court is bound to grant your request and file a formal order restoring your birth or former name. The statute is clear that you don't have to make the request in your original divorce petition. Instead, you may make your request in a separate petition, at the divorce court hearing or at any time after the divorce is final. (See Section 2, below, for instructions on restoring your name after the divorce is final.)

Once the court orders that your name is returned to your former name, your name change is complete. The court order is all the paperwork you'll need to have your name changed in other records.

2. Returning to Your Former Name—After the Divorce Proceeding

If you decide after your divorce to give up your married name and return to your birth name or other former name, there's an easy way to do it if the divorce took place in California. You can accomplish the change by filing one straightforward form with the same court that processed your divorce. Called an Ex Parte Application for Restoration of Former Name After Entry of Judgment and Order, this is a simple one-page form.

You'll find a blank Ex Parte Application for Restoration of Former Name After Entry of Judgment and Order in the Appendix. A sample is shown below.

Here are instructions for filling out the Ex Parte Application.

Caption. Fill in the caption boxes with the exact case name and number from the divorce or annulment proceeding. Pull out your divorce paperwork to be sure you've got it right.

Item 1. This line asks for the date your divorce or annulment became final. Fill in the date the court entered the final order.

Item 2. List the name you want to return to on this line.

Date and Signature. Write the date and your current (married) name, not the name you are petitioning to return to. Sign the signature line with your current name.

You are not required to send a copy of the Application to your former spouse. Just fill out the Application, file it with the divorce court and pay the filing fee. After the judge signs the form, your name change is complete. A copy of the order is your proof that your former name has been restored.

You may be able to change to a new name at divorce. The simple name change at divorce procedure, described in the California Family Code, only refers to birth or former names. This means if you want to change your name on or after divorce to an entirely different name, the court may not grant your change, since it is not required to do so. But if your divorce is not yet final, you may as well try asking the court to change your name—even if you want an entirely new name. If the court refuses to grant it, you can just file a separate name change petition (following the instructions in Chapter 6, Court Petition). In Section 3, below, we describe how to change your name if you are *not* returning to a birth or former name.

Using the Usage Method to Return to a Former Name

Because women often return to their former names after divorcing, they could traditionally make this change using the Usage method without going to court. However, DMV regulations have called this into question. The regulations require an applicant to produce official proof of a name change. Acceptable proof includes a divorce order *that lists the legal name of the applicant as a result of the proceeding.* So, if you didn't have the divorce court change your name, the DMV won't change your name on your driver's license or ID card. That's why we suggest you petition the divorce court to legally change your name. (Unless you were divorced outside of California; see "Other Circumstances," below.)

Ex Parte Application for Restoration of Former Name
After Entry of Judgment and Order

ATTORNEY OR PARTY WITHOUT ATTORNEY (Name and Address):	TELEPHONE NO.:	FOR COURT USE ONLY

ATTORNEY FOR (Name):

SUPERIOR COURT OF CALIFORNIA, COUNTY OF

STREET ADDRESS:

MAILING ADDRESS:

CITY AND ZIP CODE:

BRANCH NAME:

MARRIAGE OF

PETITIONER:

RESPONDENT:

EX PARTE APPLICATION FOR RESTORATION OF FORMER NAME AFTER ENTRY OF JUDGMENT AND ORDER	CASE NUMBER:

APPLICATION

1. A judgment of dissolution or nullity was entered on (date):

2. Applicant now requests that her former name be restored. Her former name is (specify):

Date:

....
(TYPE OR PRINT NAME)

▶ _____
(SIGNATURE OF APPLICANT)
(USE CURRENT NAME)

ORDER

3. IT IS ORDERED that applicant's former name is restored to (specify):

Date:

☐ JUDGE OF THE SUPERIOR COURT ☐ COMMISSIONER OF THE SUPERIOR COURT

[SEAL]

CLERK'S CERTIFICATE

I certify that the foregoing is a true and correct copy of the original on file in my office.

Date: _____ Clerk, by _____, Deputy

Form Adopted by Rule 1287.50
Judicial Council of California
1287.50 [Rev. July 1, 1994]

EX PARTE APPLICATION FOR RESTORATION OF FORMER NAME AFTER ENTRY OF JUDGMENT AND ORDER
(Family Law)

WEST GROUP Official Publisher	Family Code, § 2080

3. Other Circumstances

In some circumstances, a person who has gotten divorced may not be able to use the divorce process to accomplish a name change. For instance, you may have gotten divorced in a state other than California. Or, you may want to change your name to something other than a birth name or former name. In these situations, we recommend you use the Court Petition method covered in this book to accomplish your name change.

As with other name changes, you are free to try to change your name without an official decree. Because name changes after divorce are common, you may have some luck. But if you want the change to be final and complete, we recommend going to court. Again, the court petition name change process is easy, and this book will walk you through it. (See Chapter 6, Court Petition.)

C. Custody, Remarriage and Children's Names

When parents split up, their children's last name can often become an issue. For example, a common area of conflict arises when a woman who has taken her husband's name gets custody of the children. If she returns to her birth name or former name, she may want her children's last name to match hers. Or, if she remarries and takes her new husband's name, she may want her children to bear the name of her new husband.

If the child's father consents to a proposed name change, the court should grant the change without batting an eye. When both parents support a child's name change, the court will normally grant it, regardless of whether the parents are married to each other. It is a different matter, however, when one parent contests the name change. Typically, a father who continues to support and care for his child will want the child to bear his name even if the child's mother feels differently.

Traditionally, courts found that a father had an automatic right to have his children keep his last name if he continued to actively perform his parental role. No longer. (See *Marriage of Schiffman,* 28 Cal. 3d 640, 169 Cal. Rptr. 918 (1980).). Today, there are no automatics—instead, court decisions regarding children's names turn on "the best interests of the child." The court will look at all the factors in each particular case and listen to all the parties involved. What this all boils down to is that it's up to a judge to decide which name is in the children's best interest. In Chapter 6, Section A, we discuss the "best interests" standard further.

Giving a child a different name from the father's or otherwise changing the child's name does not affect the child's parental relationships in the eyes of the law. For example, if you change your child's last name to your new husband's name, your new husband does not become the child's legal father. Thus, names do not affect what the law calls "paternity" (the legally recognized identity of the child's parents).

The new husband of a woman with custody of her children cannot petition to change the children's names unless he has legally adopted them. Normally, a stepparent can adopt his spouse's child only with the consent of the child's other parent, if the other parent has abandoned the child (not visited or provided support for the child in over a year) or if the other parent has passed away.

Stepparents can handle their own adoptions using *How to Adopt Your Stepchild in California,* by Frank Zagone and Mary Randolph (Nolo).

A child's name change also does not affect the rights or duties of either parent, including visitation, child support or rights of inheritance. Only a court proceeding that changes the child's legal parents could effect such a change. Such proceedings include a legal adoption or a hearing to establish the father's identity—not a name change petition.

Although you may be able to change your own name in a divorce proceeding, you will not be able to change your child's name in the divorce proceeding. If you want to change your child's name, you'll have to file a separate court petition. For more information on how to change your child's name, see Chapter 1 and Chapter 6. ■

CHAPTER

5

Birth Certificates

When a child is born, hospital personnel or the person who delivered the baby outside of a hospital complete a birth certificate to officially register the birth. A birth certificate normally lists the child's name, the names of the child's parents and the time and place of the birth. The State Registrar of Vital Statistics keeps original birth certificates after they have been reviewed by the local health department. County health departments maintain copies of birth certificates for births in the county during the last year or two; county recorders maintain copies for all births in the county.

In rare circumstances, a child's name can be changed by having a new birth certificate issued in the new name. Section A, Children and Birth Certificates, describes all of these situations. In a few instances, a whole new birth certificate can be issued and, in others, you can receive an official amendment with new information that can be attached to the existing birth certificate.

Adults are usually unable to have a new birth certificate issued. If they want a court-ordered new name reflected on their birth certificate, they'll have to settle for an amendment which can be attached to their existing birth certificate. See Section B, Adults and Birth Certificates, for more information.

Birth Certificates and Names Are Two Different Things

If you change your name, either by usage or going to court, you do not need to change or amend your birth certificate to complete the process. In fact, in most name change circumstances people are unable to change their birth certificates. But even when people are able to change or amend their birth certificates to reflect a different name, doing so is a separate bureaucratic process from the name change itself. The only exceptions to this rule affect children and are described in Sections A1 and A2, below; in these narrow circumstances, a child's birth certificate can be changed to reflect a new name. This action also officially changes the child's name.

⚠ Only California birth certificates are covered here. This chapter describes the law of birth certificates for people born in California. If you were born in another state or country, contact that state's vital statistics department for information on changing your birth certificate.

A. Children and Birth Certificates

There are several circumstances in which a minor child can get a totally new birth certificate. When the state issues a new birth certificate, the old one is sealed, which means it can be accessed only with a court order. In other situations, a child's existing birth certificate can be amended to add new information. This section describes all of these circumstances.

1. Acknowledgment of Paternity

When a child's birth certificate lists no parents or only one parent, either the father or mother or both can file an application which acknowledges his or her paternity and requests a new birth certificate. Whether the child's natural parents were married at the time of birth, marry later or never marry, missing information about the parent(s) may be added. So long as the child's current birth certificate does not list conflicting information, the Department of Health Services will issue a new birth certificate with the updated information. (Cal. Health & Safety Code §§ 102750-102765.) At the same time, the child's name may be changed on the birth certificate to match the new information.

The father or mother acknowledging paternity must be willing to sign a statement under penalty of perjury confirming that he or she is the natural parent. The form used by the State Registrar of Vital Statistics for requesting a change to a birth certificate is the Application for Preparation of an Amended Birth Record After Acknowledgment of Paternity.

> **EXAMPLE 1:** Karen Klone and Sam Same have a child together. On the birth certificate, Karen gives the child the first name Brad and a last name she makes up on the spur of the moment. No father is listed on his birth certificate. Karen and Sam later file statements acknowledging that Sam is the father and requesting that Sam be listed on the birth certificate. They also ask that Brad be given his father's last name. A new birth certificate is issued showing Sam Same as the father, and Brad Same as the child.

> **EXAMPLE 2:** Rose Red and Omar Orange have a daughter. She is listed on the birth certificate as Shelley Red, with Rose listed as the mother and Omar listed as the father. Rose and Omar file statements requesting that Shelley's last name be changed to that of her father. A new birth certificate is issued listing Shelley Orange as the child.

> **EXAMPLE 3:** Becky Bright and Don Dark have a child before they are married. The child's name is listed on the birth certificate as Tommy Dark, but no father is shown on the birth certificate. After Becky and Don marry, they file statements acknowledging that Don is their child's father. A new birth certificate is issued listing Don Dark as Tommy Dark's father.

If a man wants to acknowledge his paternity of a child but the child's birth certificate lists another man as the father, the petitioning man can't use this simplified procedure. That's because the birth certificate contains conflicting information—the other man's name. In order to have his name put on the birth certificate, the petitioning man would have to first initiate a paternity lawsuit, as described below.

2. Judicial Decree of Paternity (Court Order)

A "paternity action" is a lawsuit to determine the father of a child. Such a lawsuit can be brought to court by the father, mother or district attorney. Many paternity actions are initiated by district attorneys on behalf of county welfare offices which provide financial assistance to families and are required by law to seek reimbursement from the father. If a court finds a man to be a child's father, the man will have a legal duty to support the child. His visitation rights and the child's rights to inherit are also affected.

If the court determines that a certain man is the father, it will issue a "judicial decree of paternity" or an "adjudication of paternity"—an order officially declaring this fact. With a judicial decree of paternity in hand, the father or mother can request that a new birth certificate be issued containing the relevant information. (Cal. Health & Safety Code §§ 102725-102735.) If another man had been listed as the father on the original birth certificate, his information will be removed and replaced. At this time, the child's last name can also be changed on the birth certificate to that of the man declared to be the father.

3. Adoption

When a legal adoption is complete, the court normally issues an adoption report, which states that the adoption is final and lists all relevant information. The adoption report will include the child's new name, assuming the court's adoption order changed the child's name. This is usual but not legally required. For instance, in the case of a stepparent adoption, an older child may or may not take the stepparent's name.

Following state law, the court forwards the report to the State Registrar of Vital Statistics no later than five days after the adoption is finalized. (Cal. Health & Safety Code §§ 102625-102710.) If the child was born in California, the State Registrar will issue a new birth certificate for the child. This birth certificate will include the child's name as it is listed on the adoption report, the time and place of birth, and the name and ages of the adopting parents. No reference is made to the adoption. If the adopting parents wish, the new birth certificate will not list the name and address of the birth hospital or the color and race of the parents. (Cal. Health & Safety Code § 102645.)

4. Gender Correction

It's possible to have a new birth certificate issued when the original lists incorrect gender information. For example, if you name your daughter Billy and somehow the birth certificate lists her sex as male, you can get it changed. Obviously, the purpose of the statute is to provide a remedy for people whose birth certificates are wrong due to an error by the birth hospital or local registrar. An application under this statute must include one of the following:

- an affidavit (a statement signed under penalty of perjury) from the administrator or representative of the birth hospital, acknowledging that the incorrect gender information is due to the hospital's error
- an affidavit from the local registrar, acknowledging that the incorrect gender information is due to the registrar's error, *or*
- an affidavit from the physician attending the birth of the applicant *and* an affidavit from a relative of the applicant who was at least five years old at the time of the applicant's birth, verifying that the applicant's gender was different at birth from that listed on the birth certificate. See the following examples of these types of affidavits.

A birth certificate issued under this statute will appear no different than an original birth certificate. (Cal. Health & Safety Code §§ 103446-103449.)

Affidavit of Steven Hart, Presiding Doctor at Birth of John Michael Mills

I am an obstetrician and have been licensed to practice in the State of California since 1961.

I presided at the birth of John Michael Mills to parents Mary Mills and Ted Mills at Beth Israel Hospital in Los Angeles, California, on March 10, 200X. Although John's birth certificate states that he is female, at the time John was born, he was male.

I declare under penalty of perjury under the laws of the State of California that the foregoing is true and correct.

Dated: _[date]_____

_[Signature of Steven Hart]__
Steven Hart

Affidavit of Melissa Mills, Sister of John Michael Mills

I am the daughter of Mary Mills and Ted Mills, and I was born on March 8, 1988.

I am the sister of John Michael Mills. I was seven years old when John was born at Beth Israel Hospital in Los Angeles, California, on March 10, 1995. Although John's birth certificate states that he is female, at the time John was born, he was male.

I declare under penalty of perjury under the laws of the State of California that the foregoing is true and correct.

Dated: _____[date]_____

_____[Signature of Melissa Mills]_____
Melissa Mills

---

5. Fixing Clerical Errors on Birth Certificates

Occasionally, errors are made on original birth certificates. Typically these are typographical errors—for example, a child's name is listed as "Nose" instead of "Rose." Sometimes an item is left blank, such as a child's first or middle name. You can correct a minor error, like these by attaching an amendment with the corrected information to your birth certificate. Although the birth certificate itself is not changed, the correction becomes an official part of the record. (Cal. Health & Safety Code §§ 103225-103255.)

Birth certificate corrections only work for minor errors. The Office of Vital Records will not accept substantial name changes using a clerical error type amendment. An example of a substantial change is completely replacing a first name—for example, changing "Mary" to "Phyllis." Other substantial changes include gender errors and paternity errors. You are eligible to obtain a new birth certificate for these types of errors—rather than merely an amendment—but you will have to fulfill more specific and rigorous requirements. (See Sections A1, above, for missing paternity informa-

tion, A2 for incorrect paternity information and A4 for gender error.)

To accomplish an amendment of a clerical error, you must also provide two affidavits—statements signed under penalty of perjury—in which the signers testify to the error. The affidavits must be completed by:

- yourself (either on your own behalf or on behalf of your child), *and*
- any other credible person with information about the error. A hospital official should complete an affidavit whenever possible. (See the sample affidavits in Section A4, above, for guidance in creating affidavits for this situation.)

Depending on the circumstances, the correct form will be either Form VS-24, "Application to Amend a Record," or Form VS-107, "Application to Complete Name of Child by Supplemental Name Report—Birth." The Office of Vital Records supplies affidavit forms, as well. (See "Forms and Assistance from the OVR," below.)

Promptly fix birth certificate mistakes.
There is no charge for correcting errors to a birth certificate if the change is made within one year of the child's birth. Also, you are more likely to have your proposed change approved if you act promptly.

6. Adding a Parent's New Name to a Child's Birth Certificate

After a parent changes his or her name, an amendment showing the parent's new name can be added to the child's birth certificate. The attachment indicates that the parent is "AKA" (also known as) and gives the new name. Adding an attachment does not change the child's name and it will not result in a new birth certificate being issued.

B. Adults and Birth Certificates

Adults can amend their birth certificates after a court-ordered name change. Most people don't bother, since amending a birth certificate doesn't legally have any affect on the acceptance of a new name, but it can be done. See Section B1, below, for more information. Adults are rarely able to have entirely new birth certificates issued. Sections B2 and B3, below, describe these circumstances.

1. Adding New Name After Court Ordered Name Change

If you were born in California and had your name changed in court, you can have an amendment attached to your birth certificate to reflect your new name. You can use this procedure after a name change by Court Petition, as well as after any other court order that changes your name, such as a divorce order or adoption. There is only one requirement: The court order changing your name must have been issued by a court in California or any other state or territory of the United States. (Cal. Health & Safety Code §§ 103400-103410.) The amendment does not actually change the content of the birth certificate itself, but it is physically attached to your birth certificate and becomes an official part of that record. The correct form for this situation is Form VS-23, the "Application for Amendment of Birth Record to Reflect Court Order Change of Name." (See "Forms and Assistance From the OVR," below.)

⚠️ **Amendments are not allowed after usage method name changes.** If you change your name by the usage method, you will not be able to amend your birth certificate to reflect your new name. A court order is required to amend your birth certificate.

2. Sex Change Operation (Court Order)

A person born in California who has undergone a surgical sex change operation may obtain a new birth certificate which lists his or her new name and gender. To do so, an applicant must first go to court and obtain an order that affirms both the new gender and new name. He or she must then file the court's order, plus the appropriate form (and fee), with the State Office of Vital Records. (See Cal. Health & Safety Code §§ 103425-103445 and Chapter 6 for more information.)

3. Offensive Racial Description

While not a name change, an applicant can request a new birth certificate if the original contains a derogatory, demeaning or colloquial racial description. To have the birth certificate changed, you must identify the term you want changed, provide an accurate racial description and pay a specified fee. (Cal. Health & Safety Code §§ 103350-103375.)

> **EXAMPLE:** Sharlene Jones was born in 1951 to an African-American father and a Caucasian mother. The attendant who filled out her birth certificate listed her race as "mulatto." Sharlene has always hated this term, but never realized there was anything she could do to change her birth certificate. When she learns that she does have a recourse, she decides she wants to change her birth certificate and that she wants to be listed as an African-American. She applies to the state and she is issued a new birth certificate.

4. Gender Corrections and Minor Errors

Adults, like children, can have their birth certificates changed if the gender is listed incorrectly or a minor clerical error occurred. See Sections A4 and A5, above, for more information.

Forms and Assistance From the OVR

The proper application forms for any of the situations discussed in this section are available by mail from the Office of Vital Records, Department of Health Services, 304 "S" Street, Sacramento, CA 95814, Telephone 916-445-2684 (recorded information) or 916-445-1719 (for assistance). You can download certain forms from the Department of Health Services website, http://www.dhs.ca.gov. Currently, the only form available online that relates to birth certificates is the Birth Certificate Request form, but you might want to check the site to see if they have added any forms since the publication of this book. Some forms are also available from local county recorders. You can submit order forms by fax to the Department of Health Services at 800-858-5553. Check in the county listing in the government section of the phone book and call for details.

6

Court Petition

A. Introduction

There is no need to hire a lawyer to successfully petition a court to change your name. A name change petition is a straightforward legal matter which non-lawyers can easily understand and accomplish. In fact, many thousands of non-lawyers have successfully handled their own name changes (many with the help of this book). As a result, courts are accustomed to seeing petitions filed by non-lawyers for name change matters.

1. An Overview of the Court Petition Process and This Chapter

If you use the Court Petition method for changing your name, you will be doing just that—petitioning (asking) a court to officially change your name. As we describe in Chapter 1, this process is quite simple. You will:

- fill out a few straightforward forms (included in the back of this book)
- file the forms with your local Superior Court
- pay the filing fee (unless you are eligible for a fee waiver)
- arrange for a local newspaper to publish a notice of your proposed change, and
- possibly, but not necessarily, appear in person before the court.

It will take a bit of time and money to complete these steps. But when you are finished, your name will officially be changed. There will be no need to hassle with bureaucrats to get your new name accepted, because you'll have a court order backing up your new name. Given the movement towards more stringent requirements for having your name changed on personal documents, exemplified by the California DMV regulations (discussed in Chapter 1), we think the time and expense you'll spend by going to court will be worth it.

Those divorced in California have an easier option. For women divorced in California, a simple one-page form, Ex Parte Application for Restoration of Former Name After Entry of Judgment, can be filed in the divorce case, even years after the divorce was final. Therefore, if you were divorced in California and want to return to a birth or former name, you don't need to use the regular Court Petition method. See Chapter 4, Section B.

This chapter will walk you through each of the name change steps. Here in this introductory section, we give you information on how to best use this chapter. We also include a brief overview on changing a child's name, since this can occasionally be more complicated than changing an adult's name. Finally, we also tell you how to access the most direct resource—your local court—for more information on changing your name.

In Section B, Getting Your Papers in Order, we describe in detail each of the forms you'll need to file for your name change petition and show you how to fill out each. We concentrate on the four basic name change forms—the ones everyone changing their name in court will need to file. Most people can do the whole job with just these basic forms. But in the following three instances you also need to complete one or more additional forms:

- if you have a low income and wish to apply for a waiver of court fees
- if you are the legal guardian of a child and are applying to change the child's name, or
- if you are applying to change your name and gender in conjunction with a sex-change operation.

After you have finished filling out your forms, you'll go on to Section C, which contains step-by-step instructions for petitioning the court. Here we'll tell you how to complete the remaining steps for petitioning the court, from filing your papers, to publishing your notice in a newspaper, to appearing before the court.

2. Filing on Behalf of a Child

Petitioning a court to change a child's name is often as easy as filing a petition on behalf of yourself. You will fill out all the same forms and take all the same basic steps. However, when the judge decides whether to grant the child's name change, she will only approve the change when it is in the child's best interest. Therefore, in situations where the other parent objects to your proposed name change, a contested hearing will be held and, depending on the fact situation, the chances of its being approved may drop substantially.

a. The "Best Interests of the Child" Standard

A court will change a child's name only when it is in the "best interests of the child." (Cal. Civ. Proc. Code § 1278.5.) Unfortunately, since this is applied on a case-by-case basis, this rather vague standard can leave plenty of wiggle room for reasonable people's opinions to differ. Some situations are more straightforward than others, however.

i. Situations in Which the Court Is Likely to Grant a Child's Petition

Here are three common situations in which a court is likely to have little difficulty approving a petition to change a child's name.

- both parents petition together (whether they are married or not)
- one parent petitions and, after notification, the other doesn't object, and
- abandonment by the second parent.

Where both of a child's parents petition the court together to change their child's name, a court is highly likely to grant the name change. This is true whether or not the parents are currently a couple.

EXAMPLE: Leila Norris and James Gold were living together but not married when they had their daughter Jasmine Norris-Gold. Now, three years later, they are ready to get married. They have decided they want to go by a new family name, Trey, in honor of Leila's grandfather. They petition the court to change all three of their last names to Trey.

EXAMPLE: Ted and Jessica Hie were divorced when their son William was three. Jessica and Ted have shared joint custody of William, even after Jessica got remarried and became Jessica Yates. Recently, Ted decided that he is going to move to the East Coast. Both Ted and Jessica agree that since William will now be spending nearly all of his time with Jessica, her second husband and their new baby, Jasper Yates, William should share their last name. Ted and Jessica petition the court to change their son's name to William Yates.

In both of these examples, the child's parents are in agreement and are petitioning the court together to change their child's name. Because both parents are present and in agreement, a court would be very likely to grant these name changes. This is true despite the fact that in the second example, the parents are divorced.

Another common situation where children's name changes are routinely approved involves parental abandonment. This most commonly happens when a father fails to visit or support a child for an extended period.

EXAMPLE: Jerri and Ben Best got a divorce after five years of marriage. Their daughter Becky was three at the time. Jerri returned to her birth name, Jerri Moran, and she was given full custody of Becky. Ben paid child support for one year, but after that, his checks stopped coming and he disappeared. After two years without contact and or support from Ben, Jerri applied to a court to change Becky's surname to Moran. The judge approved the change, finding that it was in Becky's best interests to do so.

Another common situation in which name changes are routinely approved involves a petition by one parent and no opposition from the other. With only the parent who wants to make the change appearing in court, the judge is likely to approve it as long as the petitioning parent can show that she has officially notified the parent who fails to appear of the proposed change.

EXAMPLE: Using the same people from just above, this time assume that Ben kept paying his child support and occasionally visited Becky. But after a few years, since Jerri has full custody of Becky, she thinks Becky should have her surname. She contacts Ben and he says he's fine with it—but he doesn't want to deal with the court so he won't sign any papers. Although Ben is still involved in Becky's life, the court would probably still find it is in Becky's best interest to be Becky Moran.

ii. Situations in Which the Court May Not Grant the Petition

In situations where both parents have maintained relationships with the child but one opposes the change, courts are usually reluctant to grant it. This doesn't mean a court won't ultimately approve the change—it just means the court will have to listen to both side's arguments and decide what is in the child's best interests. In making its determination, the court will consider:

- the length of time the child has used his or her current last name
- the effect of the name change on the preservation of the relationship with both parents
- the status and strength of the mother-child relationship and the father-child relationship

- the need of the child to identify with a new family unit through use of a common name
- for older children, the wishes of the child, and
- any other facts the court finds important in a given case.

The court will balance some or all of these factors to help it decide which name is in the child's best interest. Consider the following example.

EXAMPLE: Carol and Tom Tuschman were married in March and separated by May—together just long enough to get pregnant. Their baby Liz was born three weeks after their divorce was final. In mediation, they agreed to 50-50 joint custody. Carol returned to her birth name, Chen. She has been married twice before, and each time returned to Chen. Now, she wants Liz to be a Chen, like her two young boys from previous marriages. Tom wants Liz to stay a Tuschman, like his two teenage boys. Tom says that, given Carol's marriage record, she'll just want to change the baby's name the next time she marries. He also thinks that Liz should bear his name. Carol says she's willing to let Liz have a hyphenated name combining Chen and Tuschman, but since Liz primarily lives in a Chen household, it's silly for her to be called Tuschman.

This example is based on *Douglass v. Douglass*, 205 Cal. App. 3d 1046 (1988). In this case, the court agreed with the mother—reasoning that since the mother would probably be the primary caretaker, the baby should go by her name. The court ordered the baby's birth certificate to bear a hyphenated combination of the names but that the baby should go by the mother's name only. If the case were to happen today, the court might rule differently. Hyphenated names are much more common now, and a current court might approve one for all purposes and not agree with the expert witness who testified in the Douglass case that hyphenated names are "too much to saddle a child with."

EXAMPLE: Joe and Jane Evans divorced when their son Brian was two. Jane, who kept her married name, was given full custody of Brian, and Joe was ordered to pay child support. Jane stopped receiving checks six months after the divorce, no matter how often she called Joe to remind him. A year later, she couldn't even find Joe. Jane got remarried to Bill Sears and became Jane Sears. Brian, now four, thinks of Bill as his dad and of Bill's two sons as his brothers. Jane petitioned to have Brian's last name changed from Evans to Sears. She hired a process server, who tracked down Joe and served him with the papers. Joe then filed an objection with the court.

Courts will always pause and look at the facts when asked to change a child's name over the objections of one of the parents. On these facts, though, a court will likely be willing to change Brian's name despite Joe's objections. Joe has been out of Brian's life, by his own choosing, for almost half of Brian's young life. He cannot point to a strong father-child relationship. Furthermore, the mother-child relationship *is* strong, and Brian feels close with his new family. But the court's result might be different in the following situation.

EXAMPLE: Imagine that Jane and Joe divorced when Brian was ten. Joe slid out of the picture when Brian was twelve, and Jane married Bill Sears when Brian was 14. Jane and Bill immediately have a child, so when Brian is 15 he has a new sister named Jill Sears. Jane asks Brian if he wants his name to be Evans, and knowing how she feels about his father, he says yes. Jane petitions the court to change Brian's name to Sears. Again, Joe files an objection in court.

In this situation, Brian has gone by the name Brian Evans for 15 years. His father has been in his life for 12 years. So, as compared to the previous example, Brian would likely feel much more attached to the name Evans, and he probably will always think of Joe as his father and Bill as his stepfa-

ther, even though Joe hasn't contacted him in three years. Because Brian is a teenager, he probably has an opinion about the name change—which may or may not be the same as what he told his mother. A judge would likely interview Brian and see how he feels. Brian's response may be the main factor in the court's decision.

b. Notifying Interested Parties— Service of Process

Although it isn't always possible to guess how a court will decide a child's name change controversy, one thing is sure—both living parents have the right to know about their child's proposed name change. If you are the child's parent and are filing a Petition alone without the child's other parent, the court will require you to notify the other parent. You must do this even if you have sole custody of your child. Similarly, if you are the child's legal guardian, you will need to provide service of process to the child's parents or, if the child's parents are unknown or no longer alive, to the child's living grandparents. You will also need to fill out two different forms, to provide information on your guardianship. (See Section B3, Forms for Special Circumstances, below.)

This official notification is called "service of process." You "serve" the non-filing parent by giving him a copy of a legal form called Order to Show Cause. In certain circumstances, however, a court will waive the service of process requirement. If the father has abandoned his child and the mother cannot locate him, or if the father has a history of abuse, the court may not require you to serve him. (See Section C4, The Service of Process Requirement, for much more on this subject.)

3. Getting Information From Your Superior Court

The Superior Court for your county will consider and hopefully approve your name change petition. Some of the larger counties have a large main courthouse in the biggest city and several branch courts in small cities. For example, Los Angeles county has many Superior Court branches, including Santa Monica and Torrance. If there is a branch court close to you, it normally makes sense to file your papers there.

Before you get started, you'll need additional information on filing a name change petition with your local court. You can find the phone number in the government pages of the phone book or at the court's website. (Nolo, at http://www.nolo.com, provides links to Superior Court websites throughout California. Under the Free Information and Tools section of the home page, choose the Federal, State and Local Court Information link). Tell the clerk that you will be filing a name change petition and would like to know:

- The proper branch of the court for filing your papers. Tell the clerk which city or town you (or the minor for whom you are seeking a name change) live in.
- The mailing address of the court.
- The street address of the court—if it is different from the mailing address.
- The filing fee for a name change petition. (If you cannot afford the fees, you may be able to have them waived. See Section B3, below.)
- Whether you need to file any local forms (particular to your local court) along with the state's standardized name change forms contained in this book (see Section B1, below) and, if needed, the best way to get them. Specifically, ask if you need to file a Civil Case Cover Sheet Addendum. (This is a form which individual courts may require, which helps them easily see what type of case you are filing.)
- Whether there are local court rules for name changes. (Some courts have very specific re-

quirements for form preparation, service of process and attendance at hearings, in addition to the statewide rules set out in this book.)

Again, some of this information may be available on the court's website, which you can access via the Legal Information and Tools Section of Nolo's home page.

B. Getting Your Papers in Order

The forms required for a name change are easier to complete than most job applications. We can't say that filling out the forms will be fun, but it can be satisfying to do something on your own that you would otherwise pay a lawyer many hundreds of dollars to do for you.

1. Introductory Information

This section goes over basic background information you'll need to complete the forms.

a. Summary of the Four Basic Forms

The four basic forms for a Name Change Petition are:

- **Petition for Change of Name** ("Petition"), plus its attachment called **Name and Information About the Person Whose Name Is to Be Changed**—this form is your official request to have your name changed and provides the necessary background information to process your request.
- **Order to Show Cause for Change of Name** ("Order to Show Cause")—this form is used by the court to order any one who might want to contest your name change to come forward.

- **Decree Changing Name** ("Decree")—this form, when signed by a judge, will officially change your name. It is also commonly referred to as a court order.
- **Civil Case Cover Sheet** ("Cover Sheet")—this is a simple form that goes on top of the packet of forms you'll be filing. It quickly tells the court what type of case you're filing.

The Appendix contains blank, tear-out copies of these four forms.

All these forms are produced by the state for use in every county. This book contains copies of these forms, current as of January 1, 2001. You can also find them at the California Judicial Council website, at http://www.courtinfo.ca.gov/forms, or at your local Superior Court.

Be sure your forms are up-to-date. If this book is more than a year old, check to see if the Judicial Council has issued more recent forms. Go to the Council's website, listed above. Find your way to the Name Change forms and check the date the forms were updated—if the date is after 1/1/2001, print out and use those forms. Unless the forms have been seriously overhauled, the information in this chapter will still help you with the new forms—but watch for inconsistencies.

b. Tips on Completing Forms

Most forms follow a standard, fill-in-the-blanks format. Before you begin, here is some basic information you'll need to know about completing forms.

- You'll find blank, tear-out versions of all the required forms set out in this chapter in the Appendix at the back of this book. Start by making several photocopies of each. This will save you the hassle of getting your hands on a new copy or of using a bottle of White-Out if you make a mistake. (If you do need a new copy, you can just download one from the California Judicial Council's website, listed above.)
- Some forms have printing on both sides. You can copy each side on a separate piece of paper and staple the pages together before filing. If you have access to a clever copying machine, you can make two-sided copies—make sure, though, that the top of the page remains the same for both the front and back.
- All forms should be completed carefully and neatly, preferably using a typewriter. It is best to use the larger type size. Some courts may refuse to accept forms with smaller type. If you do not have access to a typewriter, the court may provide one for public use, or a local library may rent them. You can also check the Yellow Pages for typing and paralegal services; these are small companies that prepare forms for non-lawyers at a reasonable cost. (See Chapter 8, Finding Additional Help.)
- Your court will probably accept hand-printed forms if you print clearly and neatly, generally in black ink. If you want to submit hand-printed forms, call the filing clerk beforehand to make sure they'll be accepted.
- Carefully follow the instructions in this book when completing forms. Before attempting to file them, take time to compare your work against the samples provided in this book to be sure you've got it right.

Terms Used in Name Change Forms

To complete the court forms required for a name change, you'll need to know these essential terms. They are used throughout the instructions.

Present Name: The complete name that will be changed. Even if you (or the child you're petitioning for) have already been using what will be your new official name, fill in your old name when you are asked for your "present" name. If you have used a number of names over the years, read Chapter 2, What's Your Name? to help determine which name to use when asked for your official present name. List any other names you have formerly gone by after your official present name as AKAs (also known as). For example, Joanna Barkley, a.k.a. Joanna Stern.

Proposed Name: The complete new name by which you want to be known. Even if you are already using this name for many purposes, it's still your proposed name.

Person Whose Name Is to Be Changed: This is the Person whose name will change. Use the present name here—not the proposed name. If the Person has gone by a number of names (see "Present Name," above), list her present name, followed by her other names as AKAs. There may be more than one Person Whose Name Is to Be Changed per Petition—for example, a mother and a child may both be seeking name changes. For a minor (person under age 18), list the minor's name and the words "a minor" (for example, "Kevin Apple, a minor").

Petitioner: The person(s) completing the forms and requesting the name change. Although the Petitioner and the Person Whose Name Is to Be Changed are usually the same, they can be different people when, for example, an adult seeks a name change for a minor. There may be more than one Petitioner, if, for instance, a couple is petitioning together to change their child's name. Every place a form requires you to write the name of the Petitioner, write the names of all the Petitioners.

c. How to Complete the Caption

At the top of the first page of each form you'll find several boxes with blank spaces, which together are referred to as the "caption." The caption will be identical on all your name change forms, meaning you will fill it in the same way on each. Here's how.

Petitioner or Attorney. As the person filling out and filing the forms, even if you are doing it on behalf of a child, you are the Petitioner. If another person (typically the other parent in a child's name change) will be signing and filing the forms with you, that person is a Petitioner as well. Fill in your present name in capital letters, followed by your mailing address and telephone number. You may also list your fax number and e-mail address. After "Attorney For," write "Self-Represented."

Superior Court of California, County of. In capital letters, fill in the county in which you are filing your papers. In the spaces provided below, fill in the court's street address, mailing address, and city and zip code. Also fill in the branch name, if there is one.

Petition of (Names of each petitioner): Again, fill in your own present name in all capital letters. Do this even if you are petitioning to change your child's name—you are still the Petitioner.

Petition for Change of Name. This is the title of this particular form. Each form has a title, such as "Petition for Change of Name" or "Order to Show Cause for Change of Name." Leave the title as it is.

Case Number: This is the spot where the court clerk will write or stamp your case number when you file your papers. Leave this space blank for now, since you don't have a case number yet. When you file your Petition, the clerk will open a file for you and assign you a case number. If you later need to file additional papers as part of this same name change petition, you'll need to use this number carefully copy the case number from the papers you already filed.

2. Basic Name Change Forms

This section will walk you through the basic forms, line by line.

a. Petition for Change of Name

The Petition for Change of Name is your official request to the court to change your name and/or the name(s) of other person(s). This form, along with its attachment, "Name and Information of Person Whose Name Is to Be Changed," will provide the court with the facts it needs to consider your request. You can use a single Petition to change more than one person's name—such as a couple or parent and children. However, you need to fill out a separate "Name and Information" sheet for each person whose name you want to change.

i. Petition for Change of Name—First Page

Here are the instructions for filling out the front page of the Petition for Change of Name.

You'll find a blank, tear-out copy of the Petition for Change of Name in the Appendix.

Caption. Follow the instructions in Section B1, above.

Item 1. Fill in your present name here, as the Petitioner. Do not fill in your proposed name, even if you are already using it. Write your full, complete present name. Do not use nicknames or initials (unless your full name actually contains an initial that does not stand for anything).

Item 2. Fill in the present name and the proposed name of each person whose name will be changed. As discussed in Chapter 2, if the person has used more than one name, list her current official name followed by her AKAs. Use a separate line for each person, starting with (a) and working your way down. In the first blank on each line, list

one person's present name, and in the second blank of that line, list the same person's proposed name. If you are seeking to change the name of more than five persons, check the box at the end of Item 2 and type up the remaining names on another sheet of paper following this format:

"Attachment 2—Continuation of Item 2"

	Present Name		Proposed Name
(f)	John Meyers	changed to	John Dietz
(g)	Julie Meyers	changed to	Julie Dietz

Domestic violence alert. If you are a participant in the state's address confidentiality program for victims of domestic violence and stalking and you are changing your name to avoid these problems, you do not need to list your proposed new name on your forms. In each place where a form asks you to list your proposed name, you can instead state, "confidential and on file with the Secretary of State pursuant to the provisions of the address confidentiality program." (See Cal. Civ. Proc. Code §§ 1277(b), 1278(b).)

Item 3. This line states that you are asking the court to order all persons who might want to object to your proposed name change(s) to come forward. Following this request, the court will sign the Order to Show Cause that you will fill out. You don't need to do anything to this Item.

Item 4. At the end of this line, write the number of persons whose name you want changed who are not yet 18 years of age.

Item 5. This Item asks for information on the Petitioner, if the Petition is filed on behalf of a child or children. If you are not changing any minors' names, skip this Item. But if you are petitioning on behalf of a minor, mark the box that best describes your relationship and the relationship of any other Petitioner to the child. If your relationship is not described by choices (a)-(e), mark (f) and use the space provided to type a brief description of your relationship.

Item 6(a). This Item tells the court how many "Name and Information" sheets you will be attaching to this Petition. Because you need to attach a separate "Name and Information" sheet for each person whose name will be changed, this number should be the same as the number of lines you filled in at Item 2.

Items 6(b)-(f). This line refers to Items on the "Name and Information" sheet, as a way of showing that they are really a part of this form. You don't need to enter anything on this line.

ii. Petition for Change of Name—Name and Information Sheet(s)

Here are the instructions for filling out the Name and Information sheet. Complete a separate Name and Information sheet for every person whose name you are changing.

You'll find a blank, tear-out copy of the Name and Information Sheet in the Appendix.

Caption. Fill in your present name in the box labeled, "Petition Of." Leave the Case Number box blank; as noted above, the court clerk will put your newly assigned case number here when you file your papers.

Item 6(b). Check the "self" box if you are filling out this attachment in order to change your own name. Check the "other" box if you are filling it out on behalf of someone else.

Item (1). Fill in the present name of the Person Whose Name Is to Be Changed (we'll call him or her "Person" for the rest of this form). As described above, if the Person goes by a number of names, list the present name followed by the other names as AKAs.

Item (2). Fill in the proposed name of the Person.

Item (3). Fill in the Person's birthdate and check the appropriate box to mark whether the Person is younger than 18 or 18 years of age or older.

Item (4). Fill in the Person's city and state of birth—including the country if the Person was born outside of the United States (you need not be a citizen to have your name changed).

Item (5). Check the correct box for the Person's sex.

Item (6). Fill in the Person's complete current home address, including county. This must be the same county where you will be filing the name-change papers. There is no time requirement for residency—the Person may have lived in the county for one week or 20 years.

Item 6(c). Briefly state why you are seeking a name change (or why the Person is seeking a name change). Because state law holds that every adult has the right to change his or her name, the court should grant your Petition unless one of the reasons discussed in Chapter 3, Restrictions on New Names, is apparent. Just state your reason as simply as possible. In the following sidebars, we list examples of particular language you may be able to use. To make it easier to locate what you need, we have arranged them under children and adults.

Reasons for an Adult's Name Change

You may want to use or adapt the explanations below when you complete Item 6(c) of your Petition, explaining to the court why you want to change your name. Change the language of any of the examples to better suit you. If you have already been using the proposed name, you have a great reason for the name-change request, because one of the purposes of the Court Petition method is to make an official record of Usage name changes. If that is your situation, include the words "is already known by" in your explanation.

- Petitioner's present name is inconvenient, hard to spell, unappealing, embarrassing and confusing [use words that apply]. Petitioner's proposed name is convenient and [he/she] wishes to be known by this name in all [his/her] personal and business affairs.
- Petitioner's proposed name better suits [his/her] present identity. Therefore Petitioner [is already known by and] wishes to be known by [his/her] proposed name in all [his/her] social and business affairs.

- Petitioner's proposed name is an ancestral name. Petitioner [is already known by and] wishes to be known by this name in all [his/her] social and business affairs.
- Petitioner is already known by [his/her] proposed name in [his/her] profession, and wishes to be known by [his/her] professional name in all [his/her] social as well as professional affairs. [For couples] Since Petitioners are husband and wife, they wish to be known by the same last name.
- Petitioner's proposed name is her birth [or former] name. Petitioner feels her proposed name better suits her present identity and therefore she [is already known by and] wishes to be known by her proposed name in all her social and business affairs.
- [For a couple changing each partner's last name to a combination of the two names] Petitioners want to share the same last name, and their proposed surname is a combination of their two family names.

Reasons for Children's Name Changes

If you are petitioning on behalf of a child, remember that the court will grant the name change if it is in "the best interests of the child." In Item 6(c), briefly tell the court why you believe the child will be better off with a name change. Although you cannot officially change a child's name by the Usage method, be sure to mention if the child is already known by the proposed name.

- Petitioner was awarded custody of [Minor] upon her divorce on [date]. [Minor]'s natural father has failed to [regularly] make child support payments. No payments have been received since [date of last payment]. [Minor]'s father does not show parental interest in the child and has not [regularly] exercised his visitation rights since [date of last visit]. Petitioner has changed her surname [by remarriage or by returning to her birth or former name]. It is in [Minor]'s best interests, preventing embarrassment and inconvenience, to have the same surname as [his/her] mother [and stepfather, half-brother, etc.].

- [Minor's parents have both died/Minor's mother has passed away and Minor's father is unknown.] [Minor] has been living in the household of Petitioner since [date]. Petitioner is [Minor]'s [specify relationship, such as legal guardian of the person, relative or adult friend]. It is in the best interests of [Minor] to have the same surname as the Petitioner, preventing embarrassment and inconvenience.

- [Minor] is mature enough to choose [his/her] own name, and wishes to be known by [his/her] proposed name. Petitioner consents to this change of name and also prefers the proposed name.

- Petitioner was awarded custody of [Minor] upon her divorce on [date]. Petitioner has changed her surname [by remarriage or by returning to her birth or former name]. It is in [Minor]'s best interests, preventing embarrassment and inconvenience, to have the same surname as [his/her] mother [and stepfather, half-brother, etc.]. [Minor's natural father consents to the proposed name change.]

Item 6(d). Check the box that describes your relationship to the Person. If you are filing your Petition on behalf of yourself and another person, your response to this item will obviously vary on the "Name and Information" sheet you fill out for yourself and those you fill out on behalf of the others.

Item 6(e). If you are filling out an attachment on behalf of a person younger than 18, use this section to fill in the name and home address of the child's father and mother. If, as is likely, you are one of the child's parents, fill in your name on the appropriate line and write "(Petitioner)" after it. If one of the parents is dead, put the word "(deceased)" after the name. If you do not know who one of the parents is, fill in "unknown." If you do not know the address of one of the parents, write "address unknown."

If you are a child's legal guardian *and* both of the child's parents are dead, use the space after (3) to fill in the names, relationships and home addresses of known close relatives such as sisters, brothers, aunts, uncles and grandparents. If no close relatives are known, type in the words, "As far as known to Petitioner, [Minor] has no near relatives."

Item 6(f). Every adult seeking a name change must fill out and sign this declaration to state whether or not he is in state prison or on parole and whether or not he is a convicted sex offender. Check the boxes that apply to you and sign the statement. If you are in state prison, on parole or a convicted sex offender, see the following sidebar for more information on filing your Petition.

Petitioning If You Are in Prison, on Parole or a Sex Offender

If you are in state prison, the court will not hear your Petition unless you have the written approval of the Director of Corrections. Whether or not to grant you permission is entirely in the discretion of the Director. (See Cal. Civ. Proc. Code § 1279.5(b).)

If you are on parole, the court will not hear your Petition without the written approval of your parole agent or probation officer. By state law, your parole agent or probation officer must determine whether your name change would pose a security risk to the community. (See Cal. Civ. Proc. Code § 1279.5(c).)

If you are a registered sex offender (under Cal. Penal Code § 290), the court will change your name only if the court determines that granting your Petition "is in the best interest of justice" and will not adversely affect public safety. If the court grants your name change you must notify local authorities of the change within *five days*. (See Cal. Civ. Proc. Code § 1279.5(d).)

Date and Signature. You (and any other Petitioner) must normally sign and date the Petition on the last attached page.

If this "Name and Information" sheet is *not* the last attachment to your petition, you need not sign it. Instead, check the box to the right side of the page, below the signature lines, which states "Signature of Petitioners Follows Last Attachment."

If this "Name and Information" sheet *is* the last attachment, date, print or type your present name and sign in the spaces provided. If there is a second

Petitioner, he or she should do the same on the second line provided. Signing the document "under penalty of perjury" has the same effect as a sworn statement or oath, meaning you could be prosecuted under California law if you lie.

The page has space for only two Petitioners to sign. If you are filing with more than one other Petitioner, check the box to the left of the page, below the second signature line, which states "Add Additional Signature Lines for Additional Petitioners." On a separate sheet of paper, the additional Petitioners must print or type their names, and then sign and date the page. Accomplish this by following the same signature format you see printed on the printed form.

Complete a "Name and Information" sheet for each person whose name will change. If you are petitioning for name changes for more than one person, make sure you complete a separate "Name and Information" sheet for each one. Staple all attachments to the back of the Petition.

b. Order to Show Cause for Change of Name

This form is the official court document by which the court notifies (orders) anyone who may oppose your proposed name change to come forward and voice the objection. In theory at least, the public will be aware of this order because you will publish it in the legal notices section of a local newspaper once a week for four weeks. It is extremely rare for anyone to object to an adult's name change petition.

Once you've selected a newspaper for publication, according to the instructions in Section C3, below, you're ready to complete the Order to Show Cause for Change of Name. Following are the instructions for filling out this form.

You'll find a blank, tear-out copy of the Order to Show Cause for Change of Name in the Appendix.

Caption. Follow the instructions in Section B1, above.

Item 1. Fill in your present name and the name of any other Petitioner, in the space on the first line.

Items 1(a)-(e). Fill in the present name and the proposed name of each person whose name will be changed. Use a separate line for each person, starting with (a) and working your way down. In the first blank on each line, list one person's present name, and in the second blank of that line, list the same person's proposed name. If you are seeking to change the name of more than five persons, check the box at the end of Item 1. On a separate sheet of paper, type up a list of the remaining persons. Label the Sheet "Attachment 1—Continuation of Item 1." Then, starting with letter (f), list each remaining person's present and proposed name, matching the form used in lines (a)-(e) of Item 2. See Item 2 of the Petition for Change of Name, above, for an example.

⚠️ **Domestic Violence Alert.** If you are a participant in the state's address confidentiality program for victims of domestic violence and stalking and you are changing your name to avoid these problems, you do not need to list your proposed new name.

Item 2. This line states that the court is ordering all persons who might want to object to your proposed name change(s) to appear at the court and voice their concerns.

Item 2(a). Under the title, "Notice of Hearing," the clerk will fill in the date and time of the hearing and the department and room number in which it will be held. Do not fill in the information requested in the box. The clerk will complete this item when you file your documents with the court.

Item 2(b). In the space provided, fill in the court's complete street address, unless it is the same as noted in the caption above.

Item 3. In this item, specify how you will publicize this order. If your county has at least one newspaper of general circulation that has been certified to publish legal notices, mark the box at (a).

Write the complete name of the newspaper you have selected in the space provided. See Section C3, below, for information on selecting a newspaper. If your county does not have a paper that is certified to publish legal notices, check the box at (b) and ask the court clerk how to complete the following blank. See Section A3, above, for information on contacting your court clerk.

Date and Judge's Signature. The judge will sign and date the Order here. Leave these items blank.

c. Decree Changing Name

The judge who approves your name change will complete and sign the Decree Changing Name. At that point, your name change is final. Your copy of this Decree will be your official proof of your name change.

Following are the instructions for filling out the Decree Changing Name.

📄 You'll find a blank, tear-out copy of the Decree Changing Name in the Appendix.

Caption. Follow the instructions in Section B1, above.

Item 1. Leave this sentence blank—the court clerk will fill in the date and courtroom of the hearing when you file your papers.

Item 2(a)-(f). Leave these items blank—the judge will fill in the appropriate information.

Item 3(a)-(e). On these lines, fill in the present name and the proposed name of each person whose name will be changed. Use a separate line for each person, starting with (a) and working your way down. In the first blank on each line, list one person's present name, and in the second blank of that line, list the same person's proposed name. If you are seeking to change the name of more than five persons, check the box at the end of Item 1. On a separate sheet of paper, type up a list of the remaining persons. Label the Sheet "Attachment 3—Continuation of Item 3." Then, starting with letter (f), list each remaining person's present and proposed name, matching the form used in lines (a)-(e) of Item 2. See Item 2 of the Petition for Change of Name, above, for an example.

⚠ Domestic Violence Alert. If you are a participant in the state's address confidentiality program for victims of domestic violence and stalking, and you are changing your name to avoid these problems, you do not need to list your proposed new name.

Date and Judge's Signature. The judge will sign and date the Decree here. Leave these items blank.

d. Civil Case Cover Sheet

All courts will require you to file a form called the "Civil Case Cover Sheet" with the rest of your documents. This form simply lists the fact that you are petitioning to change your name so the clerk can easily see what your case is about. This form should be filed with the court at the same time as your Petition for Change of Name.

Because this form should be filled out the same way in all name change petitions, except of course for the caption information personal to you, we have filled out much of this form for you.

You can find a filled-out copy in the Appendix at the back of this book. You need only type in the following information.

Caption. Follow the directions in Section B1, above. Fill in your personal information, the court information and the Case Name as you have done on every form.

Date and Signature. At the bottom of the page, fill in the date and your present name, then sign the form.

3. Forms for Special Circumstances

The basic forms which we describe above will cover the needs of most name change applicants. In three situations, though, an applicant will need to file different or additional forms. These situations are:

- if you have a low income and wish to apply for a waiver of court fees, (see Section 3a)
- if you are the legal guardian of a child and are applying to change the child's name, (see Section 3b), or
- if you are applying to change your name and gender in conjunction with a sex-change operation (see Section 3c).

➡ Skip ahead if you don't need to file special forms. If you do not fall into one of the three categories mentioned above, you will not need to file any of the forms we describe in the next few subsections. Skip ahead to Section C.

a. Applying for Waiver of Court Filing Fees and Costs

Under state rules, the court will waive your filing fees if you have a very low income and cannot afford to pay. You do not have to be destitute, but you really must be unable to pay. Just hoping to avoid one more expense isn't good enough. According to the state's "Information Sheet on Waiver of Court Fees and Costs," you are automatically eligible for a waiver if:

- you are receiving financial assistance under SSI/SSP, CalWORKs/TANF, the Food Stamp Program and/or General Relief/General Assistance
- your income is not enough to pay for the common necessities of life for yourself and your dependents and also pay court fees, or

- your total gross monthly household income (your monthly income before taxes or deductions are taken out) is equal to or less than the amounts shown in the accompanying chart below, "Qualifying Income for Waiver of Court Fees and Costs."

Qualifying Income for Waiver of Court Fees and Costs

Use this chart to determine whether you qualify for a waiver of court fees.

Number in Family	Monthly Family Income
1	$ 894.79
2	1,209.38
3	1,523.96
4	1,838.54
5	2,153.13
6	2,467.71
7	2,782.29
8	3,096.88
Each additional	314.58

The figures on the waiver chart were taken from the Judicial Council's "Information Sheet on Waiver of Court Fees and Costs," revised March 10, 2001, and were current when this book went to press. Check with the clerk to make sure the form—and the amounts listed—are up-to-date. This information sheet, like the other forms we describe here, is available on the Judicial Council's website at http://www.courtinfo.ca.gov/forms or from you local Superior Court.

If your monthly income is higher than indicated in the chart but you nevertheless believe you can't afford to pay court fees, the court has discretion to waive your fees. But in this situation, you must provide information about your monthly expenses which demonstrates you can't afford to pay (for example, you have experienced large medical bills). A judge will review your financial situation and decide whether all or part of the court expenses will be waived.

To apply, you will fill out two forms—an "Application for Waiver of Court Fees and Costs" and an "Order on Application for Waiver of Court Fees and Costs" which will be signed by the court if your application is approved. You will also need to supply proof of each of your statements to qualify for the waiver. We describe how to fill out these forms below.

You should normally file your Fee Waiver application at the same time you file your Petition for Change of Name. Some clerks may tell you that you'll have to wait a few days for a judge to grant the fee waiver before you can file your papers. If this happens, be polite but firm. Tell the clerk that you are entitled to file your Petition immediately under Rule 985(a) of the California Rules of Court, which states, "Upon the receipt of an application [for fee waiver], the clerk shall immediately file the application and any pleading or other paper presented by the applicant." If for some reason the clerk still will not file your papers, ask to speak with a supervisor. You can read Rule 985 in full on the Judicial Council's website, listed above, in the Rules section of the site.

If you file your papers in person, allow a little extra time, since you may have to file the Fee Waiver application in a different department (courtroom) than the regular filing desk. To find out the procedure for filing fee waiver documents, check with the court clerk.

The court has five working days from the date you file to decide whether to grant your Fee Waiver application. If the court doesn't rule on your request within that period, your fees and costs are automatically waived. (Cal. R. Ct. 985(e).) When the court rules on your application, it will complete the Order on Application for Waiver of Court Fees which you already filed, making it clear whether it has granted or denied your request. If the court grants your request, it might also file an additional document called "Notice of Waiver of Court Fees and Costs." However, some courts don't use this form. If the court denies your application, you will have ten days to pay the filing fee for your name change Petition.

If the court waives your fees and costs, you will not be required to pay the filing fee for your Petition or other related court costs. However, the court waiver will *not* take care of the fees for publication of your documents in a local newspaper. You will still be responsible for that fee.

⚠ **Lottery winners and others who strike it rich later must pay.** If, after the court grants your fee waiver application but before the court rules on your Petition, your finances improve and you no longer qualify, the law requires you to notify the court and pay your fees. See Cal. R. Ct. 985(g).

i. Application for Waiver of Court Fees and Costs

This form is your official request to the court to waive your fees and costs. In it, you will explain why you cannot pay court fees and request that the court hear your name change petition despite your inability to pay.

📄 You'll find a blank, tear-out copy of the Application for Waiver of Court Fees and Costs in the Appendix.

Caption. Follow the instructions in Section B1, above.

Item 1. Check box "a" if you are unable to pay for any of the court costs, or "b" if you are able to pay for only some of the costs. In the space provided, specify which costs you are able to pay.

Item 2. Fill in your present address.

Item 3a. If you are employed, fill in your occupation, employer and employer's address. If unemployed, fill in "N/A."

Item 3b. If you are married and your spouse is employed, fill in your spouse's occupation, em-ployer and employer's address. If you are not married or if your spouse is unemployed, fill in "/NA."

Item 4. If you are receiving public assistance of any kind, check the first box.

Items 4(a)-(d). If you are receiving public assistance, check the box(es) next to the type(s) of public assistance you are receiving.

Item 5. If you checked Item 4 (public assistance), you must: (a) give your Medi-Cal number, (b) list your Social Security number or (c) provide a receipt for the benefits you checked off in Item 4. The choice of (a), (b) or (c) is up to you. The state's "Information Sheet on Waiver of Court Fees and Costs" lists the documents that will fulfill the requirements of choice (c). (Note that many of these documents will probably include your Social Security number anyway.)

➡ **If you are on public assistance and you filled in Items 4 and 5,** do not complete the rest of the numbered items on this form. Jump to the date at the bottom of the front page, print or type your present name in the space provided at the left and sign the form on the signature line. That's it.

Item 6. Check this box if you did *not* check Item 4 (receipt of public assistance) and your gross monthly income is less than the amount shown in the chart entitled "Qualifying Income for Waiver of Court Fees and Costs," above.

➡ **If you filled in Item 6,** skip Item 7, and complete only Items 8, 9a, 9d, 9f and 9g on the back of the form. Sign and date the form on the front page.

Item 7. Check this box if you did *not* check Item 4 or Item 6, but you are genuinely unable—rather than unwilling—to pay court fees and costs. If you check Item 7, you must complete the entire back side of the form.

Date and Signature. Fill in the date and your present name and sign the form.

Caption on Page 2. Fill in your name and the name of any other Petitioner filing with you. Leave the case number blank since it won't be assigned until you file your Petition for Change of Name.

Item 8. Check this box if the amount of your earnings fluctuates from month to month, such as might occur if you are self-employed and make a fair amount of money one month but little another month. If you check this item, use averages for each of the figures required in Item 9. For example, to get a monthly average of your income for the last year, add up your total earnings for the last 12 months and divide that amount by 12.

Item 9a. Fill in the amount of your gross monthly pay. This is the income you receive each month before any taxes or deductions are taken out.

Items 9b(1)-(4). Fill in the type and amount of each of your payroll deductions in the spaces provided. Then add together all of the amounts you listed and fill in the total payroll deduction amount.

Item 9c. Subtract the total payroll deductions from your gross monthly pay: Item 9a minus the total of Items 9b(1)-(4). Fill in this amount.

Items 9d(1)-(4). Fill in information about other money you get each month, such as spousal support. Then fill in the total amount of additional money you receive each month after adding together the amounts you listed in Items 9d(1)-(4).

Item 9e. Add together Items 9c and 9d and enter this amount.

Items 9f(1)-(5). Fill in the total number of people living in your home and list their names, ages, relationships to you and their income, if any. Then add up the total.

Item 9g. Total the figures in 9a, 9d and 9f to get your total household income.

➡ **Skip all of the remaining items unless you checked Item 7** on the front of this form, in which case you must fill in Section 10-12.

Items 10a-e. List the amount of cash you have, together with major assets as specified, with values.

Items 11a-n. In these items, tell how much you pay each month in living expenses. Make sure you list all of your expenses. List the total of all these expenses in Item 11n.

Item 12. Fill in this item if there is any other reason why you can't pay court fees and costs. This might include unusual medical expenses, money spent for a recent family emergency, such as funeral and burial expenses for an indigent parent or travel to visit a seriously ill relative. Only a small space is provided, so you may need to attach an additional page marked Addendum to Item 12 to provide this information. In your own words, explain why you cannot pay the court fees and costs.

ii. Order on Application for Waiver of Court Fees and Costs

This form, when signed by a judge, will be the document that officially orders your fees and costs to be waived. Following are the instructions for filling out the Order on Application for Waiver of Court Fees and Costs.

You'll find a blank, tear-out copy of the Order on Application for Waiver of Court Fees and Costs in the Appendix.

Caption. Follow the instructions in Section B1, above.

Item 2. After you fill in the caption, just list your name, the same as on the caption, in Item 2. Leave the rest of the front side of the form blank; the court clerk and judge will complete it. Then turn to the back of the form.

Caption on Page 2. Fill in your name and the name of any other Petitioner filing with you. Leave the case number blank, since it won't be assigned until you file your Petition for Change of Name.

Address Box. In the left-hand box in the middle of the page, after the Clerk's Certification of Mailing, fill in your full name and complete mailing address.

You have now completed your part of the form. The court clerk will add other information, such as the case number, when you file your documents; and the judge will complete the rest when ruling on your Application for Waiver of Court Fees and Costs.

b. Forms for Legal Guardians

If you are a child's court-appointed legal guardian, the court will want information about the child's living relatives. You will need to file a form called a "Declaration of Guardian," which tells the court about the child's family, your relationship to the child and your reasons for changing the child's name. You must also fill out a "Decree Changing Name of Minor (by Guardian)" and file both, along with the other documents described in Section B2, above.

i. Declaration of Guardian

The Declaration of Guardian form (really an attachment to the Petition for Change of Name) explains to the court your relationship with the child and the child's relationship with his or her parents. You will also use it to tell the court why the change is in the best interests of the child and will supply other information, including the names of the child's grandparents (if you are a grandparent, you will list your own name). You need to fill out a separate Declaration of Guardian for each child whose name you want to change, and attach them to the Petition. Following are directions for filling out the Declaration of Guardian.

You'll find a blank, tear-out copy of the Declaration of Guardian in the Appendix.

Caption. Because this form is an attachment to the Petition, it does not have its own full caption. In this abbreviated caption, you just need to write your name in the left-hand box.

Item 7a. Write your full name.

Item 7b. Write your complete current address.

Item 7c. In sections (1) and (2), write the name and address of the child for whom you are petitioning.

Item 7d. Use this Item to tell the court the exact proceeding in which you were appointed the child's guardian. In the spaces provided, write (1) the county of the court which appointed you, (2) whether the department was Juvenile or Probate, (3) the guardianship case number and (4) the date the appointment became final.

Item 7e. In lines (1) through (4), write the names and addresses of the child's four grandparents, if you know them. For those you don't know, write "unknown" in the name portion. For those that have died, write "(deceased)" after the name. If you don't know how to reach of them, write "unknown" in the address portion. If you are one of the grandparents, list your own name.

Item 7f. In the space provided in Item 7f, explain why you are likely to remain the guardian of the child until the child becomes an adult. If you need extra space, check the box and continue your explanation on a separate page. Title that page "Attachment 7f." (For help in completing Items 7f, 7g and 7h, see "Sample Answers for Legal Guardians," below.)

Item 7g. Use this space to explain why it is unlikely that the child's parents will regain custody of the child. If you need extra space, check the box and continue your explanation on a separate page. Title that page "Attachment 7g."

Item 7h. In this space, tell the court why the change is in the child's best interest. You can also use this space to list any other relevant information about your guardianship or the proposed name change which you feel the court should know. If you need extra space, check the box and continue your explanation on a separate page. Title that page "Attachment 7h."

Sample Answers for Legal Guardians

Here are some examples for answers to 7(f), 7(g) and 7(h), which you can use to help you formulate your responses.

EXAMPLE 1:

7(f): I am likely to maintain custody of Ann because I am her grandmother and she has lived with me since she was born.

7(g): Ann's parents are unlikely to regain custody of her, because her mother, my daughter, died of a drug overdose, and her father is in prison. He will not come up for parole for another five years.

7(h): It is in Ann's best interests to bear my family name because it is her mother's name also, and it will help her feel like she belongs in my nuclear family.

EXAMPLE 2:

7(f): We are likely to maintain custody of Matthew because we are his godparents, and we have acted as parents to him since his parents, our close friends, were killed in a car accident.

7(g): Matthew's parents will not regain custody of him because they are dead.

7(h): It is in Matthew's best interests to bear our family name since it will complete his transition into his new family.

Date and Signature. Write the date and your full name, and sign the signature line.

Guardian of. Underneath the signature line, write the child's complete current name.

ii. Decree Changing Name of Minor (by Guardian)

Instead of filing a basic Decree Changing Name on behalf of a child, as described in Section B2, above, a guardian must file a Decree Changing Name of Minor (by Guardian). Like the basic Decree Changing Name, the Decree Changing Name of Minor (by Guardian) is the document that the judge will use to officially change the child's name. When the court approves the name change, the judge will complete and sign this form. At that point, the child's name change is final. Your copy of this Decree will be your official proof of the child's name change.

You must file a separate Decree Changing Name of Minor (by Guardian) for each child whose name you hope to change. Following are the instructions for filling out this form.

You'll find a blank, tear-out copy of the Decree Changing Name of Minor (by Guardian) in the Appendix.

Caption. Follow the instructions in Section B1, above.

Item 1. Leave this sentence blank—the court clerk will fill in the date and courtroom (often called "department") of the hearing when you file your papers.

Item 2(a)-(j). Leave these items blank—the judge will fill in the appropriate information.

Item 3. On these lines, fill in the present name and the proposed name of the child whose name will be changed.

Date and Judge's Signature. The judge will sign and date the Decree here. Leave these items blank. You do not need to sign and date this form.

⚠️ **Legal guardians must also notify the child's family.** Besides filing these two special forms, you will need to notify the child's family of the proposed name change. You must serve the Order to Show Cause on the child's parents or, if the child's parents are deceased or unknown, on the child's grandparents. See Section C4, below, for more information.

c. Petitioning After a Sex-Change Operation

People who have undergone a sex-change operation have special considerations when it comes to name changes. They can get a court order that both changes their name and gender and orders the issuance of a new birth certificate by filing only one court petition and paying a single filing fee.

Some people who have changed their sex prefer to try to change their names by the Usage method, perhaps to keep the matter out of public record. Although we think trying to employ the Usage method is often more trouble than it is worth, a sex change may be one circumstance in which you can get by without a court order. This is because the DMV will change your gender on your driver's license without a court order. Instead, you file forms filled out by your doctor verifying that your sex change is complete. Since the DMV will change your gender without a court order, you may be lucky and get a clerk who will change your name at the same time. This is more likely if your name change is minor (Joseph Smith changes to Josephine Smith) and less if you choose a completely new name (Joseph Smith changes to Sandi Jones). If you don't need to go to court for any other reason (such as, for instance, to get an order to issue a new birth certificate), you may as well try and see how you do. If you're not able to change your name, you can always go to court.

To use the Court Petition method to change your name, you will use the basic forms described in Section B2, above. However, you'll need to edit the forms to include petitions to change your gender and

to issue a new birth certificate. Start by modifying the forms as described below. This may require using a bottle of White-Out and retyping or neatly printing several additional sentences. Next, follow the instructions for filling in the forms, as laid out above.

You will also need to ask your doctor (or a doctor licensed in California, if your doctor is not) to sign a written declaration stating that your sex-change surgery has taken place and specifying your new gender. Sample declarations are contained in Section C4, below. Use these samples to create one with the applicable information for your doctor to sign. All declarations must end with the words: "I declare under penalty of perjury under the laws of the State of California that the foregoing is true and correct." The doctor must sign and date the declaration.

i. Petition for Change of Name

Following are instructions for editing the Petition to include a change of gender and issuance of a new birth certificate.

Caption. White out the current title. In the empty box, type or very neatly print in a new title: "Petition for change of name and issuance of new birth certificate." Start typing at the far left side of the box, so you'll be able to fit it all in.

Item 2. White out the first line. Starting slightly higher than where the previous line was, type: "Petitioner requests that the court make an order for the issuance by the Office of Vital Records, pursuant to sections 103425-103445 of the Health and Safety Code, of a new birth certificate reflecting applicant's proposed name as *(new name)* and gender as *(male/female),* and that the court decree the following name change:"

Item 6c. Here is language you can use as your reason for your name change. "Petitioner has undergone surgical treatment for the purpose of altering Petitioner's sexual characteristics to those of the opposite sex. A declaration of *(name of M.D. certifying sex-change operation),* M.D., a physician duly licensed to practice in this state, documenting this alteration surgery, is attached as Attachment 7 and incorporated by reference."

Attachment 7. Label your doctor's declaration "Attachment 7." Staple it onto the back of your Petition.

ii. Order to Show Cause for Change of Name

Following are instructions for editing the Order to Show Cause to include a change of gender and issuance of a new birth certificate.

Caption. White out the current title. In the empty box, type in a new title: "Order to show cause for change of name and issuance of new birth certificate." Start typing at the far left side of the box, so you'll be able to fit it all in.

Item 1. White out the first two lines. Starting slightly higher than where the previous line was, type: "Petitioner *(your name)* filed a petition with this court for an order for the issuance by the Office of Vital Records, pursuant to Section 10477 of the Health and Safety Code, of a new birth certificate reflecting applicant's proposed name as *(new name)* and gender as *(male/female)* and for a decree changing name as follows:"

iii. Decree Changing Name

Following are instructions for editing the Decree to include a change of gender and issuance of a new birth certificate.

Caption. White out the current title. In the empty box, type in a new title: "Decree changing name and order for issuance of new birth certificate." Start typing at the far left side of the box, so you'll be able to fit it all in.

Item 4. Create an Item 4 in the space after Item 3. Type in the following language: "4. The Office of Vital Records will issue a new birth certificate reflecting Petitioner's name as *(new name)* and gender as *(male/female)* pursuant to Section 10477 of the Health and Safety Code."

iv. Obtaining New Birth Certificates

To actually obtain a new birth certificate, you will need to send a form requesting a new birth certificate, a certified copy of the Decree Changing Name signed by the judge and the correct fee to the Office of Vital Records. For fee information, contact the Office of Vital Records, Department of Health Services, 304 "S" Street, P.O. Box 730241, Sacramento, CA 94244-0241, Telephone 916-445-2684 (recorded information) and 916-445-1719 (for assistance). Be sure to request the appropriate form to change your name and gender on your birth certificate.

C. Step-by-Step Instructions for Petitioning the Court

Now that your papers are in order, it's time to file them with the court and get your name change application underway. In this section, we take you through the process, including:

- checking your court's local rules, which are filled with nitty-gritty requirements for how papers must be filed
- copying and filing your papers with your court
- if you are filing on behalf of a child without the child's other parent or parents, serving the Order to Show Cause on the child's relatives
- arranging to have your Order to Show Cause published in a local newspaper, and
- attending a hearing in court on your application.

1. Check Your Local Rules

Many courts adopt "local rules" governing the nitpicky ways documents must be presented. Forms that don't exactly comply with their requirements may be rejected, even though they appear to be properly filled out. Therefore, it always makes sense to check with your Superior Court's local rules to find out:

- how many copies of each document are required. Most courts require only the original, but some require an additional copy or two.
- whether documents must be two-hole punched (along the top of the page). Some courts prefer this and others require it.
- whether documents may be folded. It seems ridiculous, but some courts refuse to accept folded documents.
- whether original documents must be marked with the word "original" and copies marked with the word "copy." Some courts prefer this and others require it, and
- whether "bluebacks" are required for non-preprinted forms. A blueback is a piece of blue paper available at many office supply stores, which is stapled to the back of each separate form. If required, you should position the blueback so it hangs down just a bit beyond the end of the document. In the bottom right corner of the blueback, you should type (or neatly write) the Petitioner's name and the name of that particular document (such as, Decree Changing Name). Courts that require bluebacks, such as Los Angeles County, usually require them only for forms that are not pre-printed—so you are unlikely to need them for the basic name change forms contained in this book (Petition, Order to Show Cause, Decree and Cover Sheet). However, in some counties if you must type and file an additional document (such as an Application to Serve by Publication or an Application to Waive the Service of Process Requirement), a blue sheet may be required.

To find your court's local rules, go to a nearby law library (see Chapter 8) or go to http://www.nolo.com. Under the Court Information heading under the Legal Information and Tools section of the home page, click on Federal, State and Local.

2. Copy and File Papers With Court

Make a few photocopies of all the documents you've prepared. Even if the court requires only the original to be filed, it's a good idea to have extra copies. If you are seeking a name change for your child and the child's other parent is not signing the petition, you'll need one or possibly more extra copies of the documents. Call the Superior Court clerk and find out. (See Section A3, above, for information on calling the court clerk.) Also, if there is no newspaper that publishes legal notices in your county, you'll need to file three extra copies of the Order to Show Cause. (See Section C3, below, for information on having your Order to Show Cause published.) If a form has attachments, staple the pages together.

To file your documents, take or send them to the Superior Court clerk. Whether you file in person or by mail, be sure to include:

- the original documents
- the correct number of copies of each document, and
- the correct filing fee or your fee waiver documents. (See Section B3, above, for fee waiver information.)

If you file by mail, also include two self-addressed, stamped envelopes.

File in person if you are in a hurry. If you have left something out or made a small mistake, the clerk will tell you and you may be able to fix it right then and there. If you file by mail, you lose time while the papers are being mailed back and forth.

If you mail the documents, include an explanatory letter. (We include a sample letter below.) Regardless of whether you file your papers in person or mail them, it's a good idea to leave an extra copy (or two) of everything at home, in case the papers are lost or misplaced.

When you successfully deliver your papers to the court, the clerk will open a new file and assign your case a number. This number will be written or stamped on all of your documents. The clerk will file your Civil Case Cover Sheet form and Petition form and may also keep one or two photocopies. Any extra copies will be returned to you. They will have a stamp in the upper right-hand corner, showing the date that the original was filed.

The clerk will also assign a court hearing date for the judge to consider your case—usually about six weeks from the date you file your papers. In some larger counties, you may have to get the court date from a different person, called the "calendar clerk." If you can't appear at the date and time the clerk selects, ask the clerk for a different hearing date. The clerk will write the date, time and location of the hearing in the appropriate box on the Order to Show Cause.

In addition to filing your papers, you need to get the Order to Show Cause signed by a judge. (As discussed in Section C3, below, it can't be published until it's signed.) Your local court will probably have a procedure in place for you to accomplish this on the day you file your papers. For example, when you call the clerk for information (following the instructions in Section A3, above), you may be told that a judge is available at a certain time each day to sign orders, and that it's best to show up then. In other counties, the clerk of the court will take your Order to Show Cause and present it to a judge for signing at a later time. You can either leave a self-addressed, stamped envelope with the clerk or make arrangements to come back later and pick up the signed copy. When the judge signs the Order, the court will officially file it and you can then have a file-stamped copy published in the paper.

Your Decree Changing Name form will not be official until after your name change is approved, at which point it will be signed by the judge and filed. (This usually occurs on your hearing date.) This means that even though you hand in or mail the Decree to the clerk at the time you file your civil case cover sheet and Petition, she will keep it, but

not officially file it. In fact, at some courts, the clerk may enter your case number and then give the Decree right back to you, for you to keep until your hearing date. But for your convenience, other courts will keep the Decree in your file until your petition is approved and it's needed.

Sample Letter Accompanying Mailed Documents

November 11, 200X

County Clerk
Superior Court of California
County of San Diego
P.O. Box 128
San Diego, CA 92112-4104

Dear Clerk:

I have enclosed:

1) An original and 4 copies each of:
   Civil Case Cover Sheet;
   Petition for Change of Name (including Name and Information About the Person Whose Name Is to Be Changed);
   Order to Show Cause; and
   Decree Changing Name.
2) A check in the amount of $___ and
3) Two self-addressed, stamped envelopes.

Please have the Order to Show Cause signed; file the first three documents, set a hearing date and return date-stamped copies to me in one of the enclosed self-addressed, stamped envelopes. The second envelope is included for mailing a copy of the decree to me after it is signed at the hearing and filed.

Sincerely,

Bessie Johnson

Bessie Johnson
1 Main Street
San Diego, CA 92101
Daytime Phone: 619-555-0505

3. Arrange for Publication of the Order to Show Cause

A name change will give you the chance to get your name in the newspaper—at least, in the "Legal Notices" section, next to the want ads. State law requires a name change applicant to publish notice of the potential name change, in order to alert the public and give anyone who wants to a chance to contest the action. You'll need to publish your Order to Show Cause in a local newspaper once a week for four weeks.

Almost any daily or weekly newspaper of general circulation printed in your county is acceptable, as long as the newspaper has been certified as a "newspaper of general circulation" by the Superior Court. If the paper runs legal ads, it's certified. Call the newspapers and find their rates for publishing an Order to Show Cause for Change of Name once a week for four weeks.

Weekly newspapers often charge lower fees. Even free weekly newspapers are often certified to publish legal notices, and their publication rates tend to be significantly lower than regular daily newspapers. For example, we recently found publication rates ranging from $40 to $200 in the same county.

After you file your papers with the court, take a copy of your officially file-stamped and signed Order to Show Cause to the newspaper you have selected. Ask that the Order be published in the Legal Notices section once a week for four weeks, and pay the required fee. After the newspaper publishes the Order for all four weeks, it will prepare a form—called a Proof of Publication—in which it certifies that the Order was published. Ask the newspaper to send that statement directly to the court, with a copy to you. You should double check that the newspaper sent the statement to the court by calling the newspaper a few days after the last publishing date.

In a few rural counties, where no newspaper is published, the court will order the clerk of the court to post the Order in three public places in the county. (Cal. Civ. Proc. Code §1277.) If this is your situation, you'll need to have three extra (file-stamped) copies of the Order to Show Cause. Give these to the clerk and request the posting. Also ask the clerk to file a proof of posting in your case once the posting is complete.

4. The Service of Process Requirement

Service of process is a legal term which means officially notifying an interested person of your court case. You do this by giving that person certain legal papers.

a. When You Will Need to Serve Other Parties

You will need to serve another person or persons with your court documents for this case only in the following circumstances.

i. Adult Name Changes

Adults changing their own names will not be required to personally notify anyone—they are the only parties with a legal interest in the case.

ii. Children's Name Changes

An adult filing a name change Petition on behalf of a child will need to complete service of process in the circumstances described below.

- If the Petitioner is the child's parent and the child's other parent is alive but not filing with the Petitioner, the Petitioner must serve the other parent with the Order to Show Cause. (Cal. Civ. Proc. Code §1277(a).)
- If the Petitioner is the child's legal guardian, the Petitioner needs to serve any of the

child's living parents or, if either or both parents have died or cannot be found, to serve the child's grandparents, if living, with the Order to Show Cause. (Cal. Civ. Proc. Code §§ 413.10, 414.10, 415.10, 415.40.)

However, the Petitioner in either of the above circumstances can have the service of process requirement waived by the court if it is in the best interests of the child.

Invite the other parent to join the petition, if possible. In most circumstances, the other parent has a legal right to contest the name change if he or she disapproves. Therefore we recommend that you start any name change process with a polite conversation with the other parent, rather than surprising him or her by serving legal papers. If he or she agrees, one good option is to fill out the court papers, and send them to the other parent for his or her signature.

Of course, it's often not possible to get the other parent to agree on the wisdom of a child's name change, particularly when the other parent thinks it's a poor idea, is hostile or has essentially abandoned the child. In these instances, your best bet may be to serve the papers and hope the other parent doesn't show up. Or if he does, that the court approves the change as being in the best interests of the child (see Section A2, above).

Military parents have the right to object even after a name change is granted. If the other parent is in the military, he can contest a child's name change after it is granted if he didn't get a chance to object at the time of the hearing due to his military service.

b. How to Serve the Order to Show Cause

Where it is required, "service of process" can be accomplished in a Name Change Petition by personally delivering the papers or, in some cases, by sending the papers by mail. When the intended recipient properly receives the documents, he has been "served." There are, of course, specific and often fussy rules on exactly how service must be accomplished in order to be legally valid.

Service of process is completed by delivering the Order to Show Cause to the intended recipient (for ease, we'll assume you're serving another parent). If the other parent lives in California, you must have him personally served with a copy of the Order to Show Cause. As the name suggests, this means the papers must actually be handed to him (mailing is not good enough). If he lives outside of California, you can serve him personally or by certified U.S. mail, return receipt requested. You must have the other parent served at least 30 days before the scheduled hearing date. The Order to Show Cause must contain the date, time and location of the hearing.

The law forbids you—the person petitioning for the name change—to serve the papers yourself. However, any other person 18 years of age or older who is not signing the Petition can serve the papers for you. This means you can ask a friend, family member, acquaintance or employee. Or, for a fee, you can hire a professional process server (listed in the Yellow Pages), or in some counties, the marshal, constable or sheriff's deputy to serve the papers. The court clerk should be able to tell you whether law enforcement officers serve civil court papers in your area (in some larger counties, they are too busy to accept this work). If the answer is yes, ask for information about fees and procedures.

After you complete service, you will need to file a short form called a "Proof of Service of Order to Show Cause," which is your proof that service was completed. First, have it signed by the process server (the person who completed service); then file it with the court that is hearing your case.

i.   Personal Service (Inside California)

To complete personal service, the adult making the service must correctly identify the recipient and hand him the papers, making it clear that they are court documents. No magic words are required—it's fine to say "These court papers are for you," or "You have been served." If the recipient won't accept the papers, the process server should put the papers on the ground as close as possible to the other parent's feet, and leave. Process is complete whether the process server is able to hand him the papers or just put them down near him. It doesn't matter if the other parent refuses to take the papers, gets angry or even tries to run away. At this point, the process server's job is done.

Your server should understand that the papers must be served on the intended recipient himself, not on a friend or family member. Usually it's best to serve the person at home, so as not to interrupt him at work. Personal service is not complete if the papers are left, for instance, on the porch, in the mailbox or with anyone except the other parent.

Never use force. Under no circumstances should the process server pick up the papers once she has put them down. If she does, the service will be invalidated and have to be attempted again. Also, she should never try to force the other parent to take the papers—legally, it's completely unnecessary and may even result in a fight and possibly a subsequent lawsuit.

You will need to give the process server copies of the Order to Show Cause and the date by which service must be completed (30 days before the scheduled hearing date). Unless the process server is familiar with the person being served, you'll need to help out by providing as much detailed information as possible, such as the best hours to find the other parent at home and a physical description. It's best if you can provide the process server with a recent photograph of the other parent.

ii.   Service by Mail (Outside of California)

If the other parent lives outside of California, you can serve him by mailing the Order to Show Cause form by pre-paid first-class mail, return receipt requested. You must mail the Order form at least 40 days before the hearing. Like personal service, you cannot complete service by mail on your own. Another adult must actually hand the envelope to a postal employee. This type of service is valid only if the other parent signs and sends the receipt back to you.

If the other parent signs for the documents, you will receive your return receipt back in the mail. Keep the signed return receipt in a safe place. You will need to file it along with a proof of service, following the instructions below.

If the other parent refuses to accept the certified envelope, you will need to:

- arrange for personal service (see above), or
- request that service be waived (see Section c, below).

iii.   Complete and File Proof of Service

Once the other parent has been served, whether in person or by mail, the person doing the serving needs to file a Proof of Service. This form is a declaration by the process server stating how and when the documents were served. Following are directions for completing the Proof of Service.

You'll find a blank, tear-out copy of the Proof of Service of Order to Show Cause in the Appendix.

Caption. Follow the instructions in Section B1, above. Carefully copy the case number from papers you've already filed.

Item 1. Leave this item blank. It simply states that the person who served the documents is at least 18 years old and is not a party to your name change Petition.

Item 2. Fill in the business or residence address of the person who served the documents.

Item 3a. Check this box if the other parent was personally served. If the other parent was served by mail, skip this item and go on to Item 3b.

Items 3a(1)-(4). Fill in the name of the other parent, the address where he was served and the date and approximate time of service.

Item 3b. Check this box if the other parent lives out-of-state and service was completed by mail. Skip this item if you filled out Item 3a (the other parent was personally served), and go on to the Date and Signature line.

Item 3b(1). Leave this item blank. It simply states that the process server mailed notice of the hearing to the other parent by pre-paid, first-class mail, return receipt requested.

Items 3b(2)-(5). In the lines provided, fill in the name of the other parent, the address to which the Order to Show Cause was mailed, the date it was mailed and the city and state from which it was mailed.

Date and Signature. The process server must fill in the date and his or her full name and sign the form on the signature line.

At least one week before the scheduled hearing date, file the Proof of Service with the court. Remember to keep copies for your file.

c. If You Can't Find or Don't Want to Serve the Other Parent

If you believe that attempting to service the other parent is useless (because she never signs for mail, for example), or you have a good reason for not wanting to serve the other parent (she has attacked process servers in the past), the court may waive the notice requirement. Or, if you are unable to locate the other parent, the court may allow you to serve the other parent by publication, which requires publishing the Order to Show Cause in a newspaper. In each of these circumstances, you will need to file an application with the court. Because the court will need time to process your request, the hearing date for your name change Petition may end up getting postponed.

Start by calling the court clerk and describe your situation. Ask whether you should apply to have notice waived or to have service by publication approved. Depending on the clerk's answer, you should file either a form entitled Application and Order for Publication or an Application and Order Dispensing With Notice.

i.   Service by Publication

If you cannot come up with an address for the other parent, you will be unable to serve him in person or by mail. In this case, the court may allow you to simply publish the notice in a newspaper in the county where the other parent is most likely to be. This is called service by publication, and consists of publishing a copy of the Order to Show Cause form or, in some counties, a local notice of hearing form, in a newspaper.

The court will allow you to serve by publication only if you cannot find the other parent after making a real effort. You may search for the other parent by yourself, but you should also try to enlist help from others, such as adult friends or relatives. Keep a written record of your search and include everything you did and everyone you contacted to try to locate the other parent, including the date of every action. Keep copies of any letters you send. Courts often require that you contact these sources:

- **Telephone Company.** Check telephone directories and directory assistance in cities where the other parent has lived recently. Most public libraries carry copies of telephone directories for many large cities, including areas outside of California.
- **Friends, Relatives and Former Employers.** Contact the other parent's relatives and friends to see if they have leads on his whereabouts. If you know where the other parent used to work, contact former employers to find out if they have an address, telephone number or the name of someone else who might know how to locate the other parent.

- **Last Known Address.** If the other parent has moved and left a forwarding address, you can obtain it from the U.S. Post Office. Send a post card or envelope to the last known address with the words "Address Correction Requested" printed next to the old address, and list your return address on the envelope. You might check with the people living at the other parent's last known address and the neighbors on both sides. If the last known address is a mental or penal institution, find out whether the institution's records are confidential or if you can obtain the other parent's current address.
- **Military Services.** If you think the other parent is a member of the military, write to the personnel records branch of the appropriate military branch in Washington, D.C. You'll need to pay a fee (approximately $15) and request information as to whether or not the other parent is on active duty in that branch of the military service.
- **Internet Services.** Although it's unlikely that a court will order you to use such a service, a number of Internet companies, including http://www.USSearch.com and http://www.peoplesearch.com, offer people locator services. For a fee, the company will search a number of public records for you. The fees will vary depending on how narrow or wide your search is.

Before the court will allow you to serve by publication, you will need to file two forms. First, you need to prepare and file a Due Diligence Declaration, in which you let the court know what steps you took in your search. (If anyone helped you with your search, you'll need to prepare a separate declaration for each person regarding what that person did and have him or her sign the document.) Second, you must file an Application and Order for Publication. In this form, you officially ask the court to allow you to serve by publication. If the court grants your application, the court will sign the form, which will serve as the court's official order.

In the Appendix, you'll find a blank sheet of pleading paper (paper with line numbers down the side). Make copies of this sheet and use them for typing up your own papers.

Use the sample Declaration and Application and Declaration, shown below, as your guides for your own papers. After you're done, make copies of the documents and file them with the court according to local rules. These rules will tell you when to file your forms—usually at least several days before the hearing date. The rules will also tell you the proper format for the forms; for instance, you'll need to check to see if there are any footer or blueback requirements. (See Section C1, above.)

Pay attention to details. Preparing any court form requires focus, but isn't difficult. Allow time and energy to carefully complete all the steps and you'll be surprised at how easy it is to do this on your own.

If the court grants your application, you will need to file the Order to Show Cause or your court's Notice of Hearing form in a newspaper that the other parent is at least theoretically likely to see. For example, if the other parent was last heard of in San Diego five years ago, you should publish there. The court will probably need to postpone your hearing date so you have time to do this, meaning you'll need to make sure the Order to Show Cause lists the postponed hearing date before you publish it. Follow the basic instructions for publishing the notice set out in Section C3, above. Again, local rules for this procedure vary, so check with your court clerk or read the local rules yourself.

ii.   Waiver of the Notice Requirement

To get the court to dispense with (waive) the requirement to notify the other parent of your child's name change, you'll have to convincingly explain to the court exactly why you believe service is not necessary.

1 [YOUR NAME in caps]
2 [your street address]
3 [your city, state and zip]
  [your phone number, including area code]
4 Petitioner In Pro Per
5
6
7
8
9 SUPERIOR COURT OF CALIFORNIA
10 COUNTY OF [COUNTY in caps, followed by branch name, if any]
11 In the matter of the application of:) Case No. [Case No.]
)
12 [NAME OF APPLICANT(S) in caps:) DECLARATION OF DUE DILLIGENCE
13 indicate if applicant is a minor]   )
)
14 I, [your name or name of person who searched for missing parent], declare that I am [if you
15 the Petitioner in this case" or state relationship, such as "the sister of Applicant and friend of Petitioner"]. I
16 have made the following attempts to locate [name of missing parent], who is
17 Applicant's ["mother" or "father"], but to date my efforts have been unsuccessful.
18   1. I checked in telephone directories for listings. The details of my
19 attempts are: [list the date each attempt was made, the city of the telephone directory and the results of the
20 search, such as no one was listed under that name, or you called and it was the wrong person].
21   2. I checked with directory assistance. The details of my attempts are:
22 [list the date each attempt was made, the city or area code that was called and the results of the search, such as
23 no one was listed under that name, or you called and it was the wrong person].
24   3. I checked with friends and relatives. The details of my attempts are:
25 [list the date each attempt was made, the name and relationship to the missing parent of each person contacted
26 and the results of the search, such as a friend didn't know the whereabouts of the missing parent, or a brother gave a
27 disconnected telephone number for the missing parent].
28   4. I checked with former employers. The details of my attempts are: [list

-1-

DECLARATION OF DUE DILIGENCE

---

1 the date each attempt was made, the name of each former employer contacted and the results of
2 the search, such as the former employer had fired the missing parent and didn't know where
3 he'd gone, or the former employer had the forwarding address of a business that went bankrupt
4 two years ago].
5   5. I checked the last known residence address. The details of my attempts
6 are: [list the date each attempt was made and the results of the search, such as you went to
7 the house and the missing parent was no longer living there and the tenant didn't know where he
8 had moved, or the post office did not have a forwarding address on file].
9   6. [List information about any other search attempts, including the date each attempt
10 was made and a detailed description of the results of the search, such as you checked with the
11 Army and there was no forwarding address on file, or you checked with the court where the
12 missing parent had filed a lawsuit and there was no current address listed in the court's
13 files].
14   I declare under penalty of perjury under the laws of the State of
15 California that the foregoing is true and correct.
16
17 Dated: [today's date]   [your name or name of person who searched for missing
18 parent].
19
20
21
22
23
24
25
26
27
28

-2-

DECLARATION OF DUE DILIGENCE

1   [YOUR NAME in caps]
    [your street address]
2   [your city, state and zip]
    [your phone number, including area code]
3
    Petitioner In Pro Per
4

5

6

7

8   SUPERIOR COURT OF CALIFORNIA

9   COUNTY OF [COUNTY in caps, followed by branch name, if any]

10

11 In the matter of the application of:)   Case No. [Case No.]
)
12   [NAME OF APPLICANT(S) in caps;   )   APPLICATION AND ORDER FOR
     indicate if applicant is a minor]   )   PUBLICATION RE: CHANGE OF NAME
13 _____)

14   Application is hereby made for an order directing service of the ["Order to

15 Show Cause" or "Notice of Hearing," depending on local rules] by publication in [name of

16 newspaper] , which is a newspaper of general circulation in this state most

17 likely to give [full name of other parent] notice of the pendency of this proceeding.

18   The whereabouts of [full name of other parent] are unknown to the Petitioner.

19 Attempts to locate [him/her are set out in detail in the Due Diligence

20 Declaration(s) filed in support of this application. Petitioner requests that

21 the court issue its order directing service of the ["Order to Show Cause" or "Notice

22 of Hearing," depending on local rules] on [full name of other parent] by publication in [name of

23 newspaper] once a week for four successive weeks as provided in Section 415.50

24 of the Code of Civil Procedure.

25 Dated: [today's date]

26
                                    _____
                                      [your   name]
27

28
                                   -1-

To apply for a waiver, prepare an Application and Order Dispensing With Notice. This document is both your formal request to the court to waive notice and, if the judge agrees and signs the paper, the court's official order waiving notice. In this form, your job is to explain concisely and compellingly why the court should not require you to notify the other parent. To succeed, you must convince the court that service would be impossible or useless. Waiver will not be approved where service is simply inconvenient.

Unlike most other forms regarding name changes, there is no pre-printed form for this. You'll have to type up your own form using the sample below as a guide.

Following is some sample language you can use or modify.

- *[Child]*'s father is unknown. He is not listed on *[Child]*'s birth certificate, a copy of which is attached to this document and incorporated herein.
- *[Child]*'s father and I were divorced on *[date]* and I do not know his whereabouts. He was denied visitation rights to *[Child]* on the basis of prior abuse and neglect, and he has had no contact with [him/her] since that date. A copy of the divorce decree is attached to this document and incorporated herein.
- *[Child]*'s father has had no contact with *[Child]* since *[specify date]*, and has not made child support payments since *[specify date]*. I have remarried, and *[Child]* is known by the last name of my husband, *[specify date]*. He has acted as a father to *[Child]* since *[specify date]*.

If you want to have the notice requirement waived because you cannot locate the other parent, you should also file a Due Diligence Declaration with your application. This form, which we described in the previous section, should tell the court everything you have done to attempt to locate the other parent. Use the sample in the prior section as a guide. If you decide to file a Due Diligence Declaration, tell the court in your Application and Order Dispensing With Notice that you are doing so. Be-

low, you'll find a sample Application and Order Dispensing With Notice.

There aren't pre-printed forms for this. You will need to type these forms up yourself. Use the sample below as a guide and type yours on copies of the pleading paper in the Appendix. Be sure to complete the forms and file them according to the requirements laid out in your county's local rules.

5. Appear in Court, If Necessary

For your final step, you may need to briefly appear in court at a hearing on your Petition for Change of Name. This is usually a very quick and simple proceeding. Often, in fact, unless someone has filed papers opposing your name change, the court is unlikely to hold a hearing at all.

a. Find Out If the Court Is Holding a Hearing

A day or two before the scheduled hearing date, call the court clerk. Explain that you have filed a name-change petition and give him your case number and scheduled hearing date. Ask the clerk:

- whether any written objections have been filed (in 99% of cases the answer will be no), and
- whether the court will be holding a hearing.

Again, if all your paperwork is in order and there is no opposition, chances are good the court will grant your name change without holding a hearing. (Cal. Civ. Proc. Code § 1278.) But in a few counties, courts may require a hearing even if there is no objection. Skip the remainder of this section if you do not need to appear in court.

If you learn from the court clerk that you do not need to appear in court, skip ahead to Section 6.

```
 1    _[YOUR NAME in caps]_
      _[your street address]_
 2    _[your city, state and zip]_
      _[your phone number, including area code]_
 3
      Petitioner In Pro Per
 4

 5

 6

 7

 8                         SUPERIOR COURT OF CALIFORNIA

 9              COUNTY OF  _[COUNTY in caps, followed by branch name, if any]_

10

11    In the matter of the application of:   )   Case No. _[Case No.]_
                                             )
12    _[NAME OF APPLICANT(S) in caps;_       )   APPLICATION AND ORDER DISPENSING
      _indicate if applicant is a minor]_    )   WITH NOTICE RE: CHANGE OF NAME
13    _____)

14         Application is hereby made for an order dispensing with notice to  _[full name_

15   _of other parent]_ , the  _["mother" or "father"]_ of minor Applicant  _[minor's present name]_ in

16   this name change proceeding. The whereabouts of  _[full name of other parent]_  are

17   unknown to the Petitioner. Attempts to locate  _[full name of other parent]_  are set out

18   in detail in the Due Diligence Declaration(s) filed in support of this

19   application. Petitioner requests that the court issue an order dispensing with

20   notice to  _[full name of other parent]_ .

21   Dated:  _[today's date]_

22                                            _____
                                                       _[your name]_
23

24
           IT IS THE ORDER OF THIS COURT that notice to  _[full name of parent]_ , the
25
     _["mother" or "father"]_ of Applicant  _[minor's present name]_ , be dispensed with.
26
     Dated:
27                                            _____
                                                   Judge of the Superior Court
28
```

b. Prepare to Attend the Hearing If Required

If you have to appear in court, make sure you know where and when the hearing will be. Bring with you:

- copies of all documents you've filed, as well as a copy of the Proof of Publication, if the newspaper sent you a copy; although the judge will have the originals, it's a good idea to bring along copies just in case
- several extra copies of the Decree Changing Name form
- copies of any final divorce decree and modification of support documents, for those petitioning to change a child's name without the consent of the other parent. Also prepare and bring a written record showing the dates of the other parent's support payments and visits to the child. Again, as discussed in A2, above, a court is more likely to find that a proposed name change is in the best interests of a child if the other parent has not supported or visited.

If you can't make the scheduled court hearing, you may be able to arrange for a "continuance"—a rescheduling—by contacting the court clerk. Courts have different procedures for arranging continuances. For example, you may need to send a letter to the court confirming the new date. Also, if anyone has filed an objection to a proposal, you'll need to formally notify that person of your request for a continuance. Especially if he or she won't go along with your request, it's even possible that you'll have to appear in court (bring a motion) to formally request the continuance.

c. Attend the Court Hearing

On the day of the court hearing, plan to arrive at the courthouse at least half an hour before your scheduled hearing. Courtrooms are often called "departments." To find out which courtroom or department you need to go to, look for a posted list outside or just inside the clerk's office—each case on schedule for that day will be listed under a certain department or courtroom. Your court may use a master calendar system whereby lots of cases are assigned to one big courtroom and then are assigned to other judges from there. If you are confused, ask the court clerk for help. Once you've found the correct room, it's good to let the courtroom clerk (sitting in front of the judge) know that you are there. There will be other cases scheduled for the same time as yours, so don't worry if you are not called right away. You can check with the clerk or bailiff or perhaps on a bulletin board to find out where you are placed on the schedule.

Once you are sure you are in the right place, sit down and watch the cases ahead of you, so you get a feel for the procedure. Above all, don't be intimidated by all the lawyers milling around. You should have no problem handling this hearing on your own.

If you are petitioning on behalf of a child, state law does not require you to bring the child to the hearing. However, your court's local rules may require the child to attend, and you should check these rules to be sure (see Section C1, above). Either way, it is usually best to bring the child, especially if the child is old enough to have an opinion about the name change.

i. Uncontested Case

Again, most courts do not require a court appearance unless objections were filed to the proposed name change. But local rules vary, and sometimes judges want to formally consider the name change in court even if no one has objected. Bear in mind that the judge must grant your request unless there is a good reason for denial, so you will normally just state your request with no need to convince the judge of anything. Here's how a court hearing will normally work.

You will be sitting in the courtroom, listening to other cases, when finally the bailiff calls the number and name of your case. For example, you may hear,

"Case Number 01-3413, In re Coughlin" or "Application of Coughlin." Rise and step forward past the little fence or wall that separates the spectators section of the courtroom from the judge's area.

In large counties, the courtroom clerk will normally ask you to take the witness stand and you will be sworn or, if you wish, affirmed ("to tell the truth," etc.). You may be asked to "stipulate" (agree) for your case to be heard by a commissioner instead of a judge. A commissioner is a well-paid court official and looks like a judge. For purposes of a name change, a commissioner has the same authority as a judge and you will want to sign the stipulation.

Call the judge or commissioner "Your Honor." The judge or commissioner will normally ask you a few questions to become better informed about your petition. For example, "Ms. Coughlin, you have petitioned this court to change your last name to Peters. You state that you are already going by this name. How long have you done so? Why have you begun to use this name?"

Answer the judge's questions briefly. For example, "Yes, Your Honor, I have been using the name Peters for three years," or, "Your Honor, after I divorced my former husband, I planned to continue to use his last name. But, later I wanted to use a different last name. I decided to go by Peters," or, "Your Honor, Peters is the family name of my maternal grandmother. I was close with her as a child, and I decided I would like to honor her and feel close to my heritage by using her name."

Ask for help if you need it. Judges are generally helpful to people acting as their own attorneys for name changes. But feel free to ask the judge or commissioner to explain any questions you don't understand.

When the judge is satisfied that the name change should be allowed, she will say something like "Granted," or "So ordered," and sign the Decree Changing Name. You say, "Thank you, Your Honor," and step down.

ii. Contested Case

If anyone files written objections to your name change, you'll need to appear in court. You should receive a copy of the written objections at the mailing address you put on your petition. If you don't receive an objection, but suspect one is likely to be made, go to the clerk's office and ask to see your file. If an objection is on file, you can get a copy for a small fee.

Anyone who files a written opposition to your Petition must state a specific reason for the objection. Most objections are for one of the reasons listed below.

- A relative may object who does not approve of a minor's proposed name change. For example, a natural father doesn't want his child's name changed to the stepparent's last name or mother's birth name.
- A prominent person with a name similar to your proposed name may object, claiming you intend to impersonate her or otherwise capitalize on her name.
- A creditor who suspects you want to change your name to try to avoid paying your debts objects to your proposed change.

If you face a contested name change, you may wish to arrange for a lawyer to represent you. If so, you'll probably want to emphasize that you've already done all the paperwork and simply want to be represented at the hearing. This shouldn't involve more than a few hours of work, so the fee should be modest. (See Chapter 8.)

However, you should also consider representing yourself, especially if the written objection isn't substantial and can easily be countered. For example, if someone with a name similar to your new name objects, claiming you want to impersonate her or steal her identity, you will need to tell the judge your legitimate reason for the change. This is not akin to splitting the atom. Just be prepared to explain how you decided on the name—maybe it was your uncle's name or your sister has called you by this nickname since birth. Perhaps the name you've chosen is similar to the objector's name only by co-incidence.

A contested case proceeds pretty much the same way as an uncontested case. You will be sworn in to tell the truth. The court may ask you to testify from the witness stand, as if you were a witness at a regular trial. The judge will give you a chance to state your reasons for the name change. The judge may help you do this by asking pertinent questions, or may simply ask you to proceed. To deal with the possibility that the judge may not be particularly helpful, you'll want to be prepared to make a short statement as to your key reasons that your proposed name change should be approved. In some situations, after you have finished, the court will call on the person opposing the name change to voice her objections. After this is done, you'll normally have a chance to reply.

Let's take a look at a couple of examples to see how the process works. Kristophos Yukabonkerz-kapowpolis (we'll call him "Kris") files a petition to change his name to Kris Kapow. Unfortunately for Kris, two written objections are filed, one by Cruz Creditor, to whom Kris owes $3,000; and another by Chris Capow, a famous Hollywood stuntwoman who specializes in being shot out of cannons. Cruz thinks Kris wants to use his new name to avoid re-paying his debt, and Chris is afraid Kris will try to profit from his similar-sounding new name. Here's what Kris says upon being sworn in and taking the witness stand.

"Good morning, Your Honor. I currently use the name Kris Kapow, and I am petitioning the court to approve my use of this new name, from my former name, Kristophos Yukabonkerzka-powpolis. I want to change my name because my present last name is obviously very difficult to pronounce and spell. And because it just plain won't fit on the back of my uniform. I am a college football player and hope to turn pro next year. I do not propose this new name in or-der to avoid any debts, including the one to Mr. Creditor. I am fully aware that a name change has no legal effect on this or any other debt and

am willing to make this clear in writing to Mr. Creditor.

"As to Ms. Capow's objection, I do not intend to use my new last name to profit from her identi-cal-sounding last name. In fact, before she filed her objection, I had never heard of her. My own occupation as a football player is quite different from hers. I chose the new name "Kapow" be-cause that word is contained in my much longer birth name. Out of pride in my ethnic heritage, I wish to retain a small part of that name."

Hannah Morton has petitioned to change her young daughter Cynthia's last name from Davis to Morton. Hannah's ex-husband and Cynthia's father, John Davis, has not contacted either Hannah or Cynthia for the last 18 months—since Cynthia was two. After Hannah served John with the Order to Show Cause in this case, John filed an objection with the court. He says that he is still Cynthia's father so she should bear his name. He claims that he has been out of work for over a year, so he couldn't make child support payments and was embarrassed to contact his daughter. Here is what Hannah says to the court:

"Good morning, Your Honor. My name is Hannah Morton. I am the mother of Cynthia Davis, and I am petitioning the court to change Cynthia's name to Cynthia Morton. Currently, Cynthia bears the family name of her father, John Davis. Mr. Davis and I were married when Cynthia was born, but we were divorced two years later. In the divorce decree, I was given full custody of Cynthia because the court found that I could provide Cynthia with a more stable and nurturing environment than Mr. Davis could. The court granted Mr. Davis visitation of two weekends per month with his daughter, and the court ordered Mr. Davis to pay me $1,000 per month for Cynthia's care. I have filed a copy of the divorce order in this case, but I have a copy here if the court needs it.

"Mr. Davis made his required payments for six months. During that time, he visited Cynthia about once per month and each visit was only for a few hours, rather than an entire weekend. After those six months, Mr. Davis stopped contacting us and did not send any more child support payments. I tried to call him but he did not return my calls. Since that time, I have had to take a second job to support myself and Cynthia. It has been hard, but I have still provided Cynthia with a loving and nurturing environment. Although Mr. Davis will always be Cynthia's biological father, he has not shown himself to be a reliable parent and has chosen to not be a part of her life. I love Cynthia very much, and because I am her sole caretaker, I believe she should bear my family name."

After hearing your reasons and any objections, the judge is likely to grant or deny your Petition right then and there. However, especially if a child's name change is involved and emotions are running high, the court may tell you it is taking the matter "under submission" or "under advisement." This is legal jargon for "I'll think about it and tell you what I decide later." If so, the court will notify you by mail of its decision. If you don't hear within a week or so, call the clerk and find out what the court has decided or when it plans to decide.

6. After Your Name Change

When the court grants your name change petition, and signs your Decree, your name change is legally complete. You may want to take a few more steps, however, to make your new name widely known.

- **Obtain a Certified Copy of the Decree.** Some agencies or organizations won't ratify your change without a copy of the Decree officially certified by the court clerk. For a small fee, the court will certify a copy of the Decree for you. You can obtain a certified copy in person or by mail—talk to your court clerk for information.

- **Amend Your Birth Certificate.** After a court-approved name change, you can amend or, in some cases, change your birth certificate to reflect your new name. See Chapter 5, Birth Certificates, for more information.

- **Notify Agencies and Institutions.** If no one knows about the name change, it won't do you any good. Turn to Chapter 7 for information on how to notify people, institutions and government agencies of your new name. ■

How to Get Your New Name Accepted

The most important part of accomplishing a name change is having public agencies and private businesses accept your new name. If your IDs and records still list you under your old name, your name change obviously isn't complete. Although it may take a little time to contact government agencies and businesses, don't be intimidated by the task—it's a common procedure. For example, thousands of women who take their husbands' name when they marry do essentially the same thing every day.

There are three practical steps to implementing a name change.

- Use only your new name. This is especially important if you are changing your name by the Usage method; as discussed in Chapter 1, Section A, a Usage method name change is legally valid only if you use your new name in all aspects of your life.
- Tell your friends and family to call you by your new name only. This change may be the hardest. It will probably take a while for those close to you to make the switch, and
- Inform the various government agencies and businesses that you deal with of your name change. See Section B, below, for help with this process.

A. Documentation

In this section, we discuss the paperwork that shows the world that your name has been changed. This documentation will be important when you try to change records and obtain identification in your new name.

1. Court Petition and Other Court Order

If you changed your name by going to court, either by filing a name change Petition or including a name change in another proceeding, you already have official documentation of the change: either the Decree Changing Name or divorce or adoption court order changing your name. The document shows that the state has recognized your name change.

Armed with your court order, it will be very easy for you to have your new name accepted. Show this to agencies and institutions that require proof of your name change. Note that a few agencies may want to see, and perhaps keep, a certified copy or your Decree or other order.

If you are changing your name on getting married, your marriage license will serve as your "official" documentation of your name change. Although the certificate does not officially change your name, most agencies and businesses will accept it as proof of your change.

2. Usage Method

Changing your name by the Usage method doesn't require or create any court-ordered documentation of the change—all you have done is started using the name. However, it may be helpful to prepare your own written statement of the change.

When dealing with agencies and businesses, it's often helpful to have something in writing. It is also a useful way to remind them that it is legal to change your name by the Usage method. They may resist changing records to your new name, and often you must deal with someone who is not allowed to take your word for anything.

There's another reason for preparing a written statement now. Sometime in the future, you may need documentation showing when you started using the new name. For example, after changing your name by Usage, you must wait five years before you can get a passport listing only your new name.

Below you'll see samples of an official-looking form that you can use to declare your name change (these are not California court forms, but ones we designed in order to accomplish this purpose). If you are changing to a new name altogether, use the

Declaration of Legal Name Change; if you are changing to a formerly used name, use the Declaration Restoring Former Legal Name.

The Declaration states that you have taken on a new name as of a certain date. We recommend that you have this form notarized, though this step is not a legal requirement, because it demonstrates you are serious about the name change. This involves showing the notary a piece of identification, such as a driver's license, then signing the document in front him. You can locate a notary public in the Yellow Pages or through some banks and real estate offices. Notaries charge varying fees, often around $10.

You'll find blank, tear-out copies of the Declaration of Legal Name Change and the Declaration Restoring Former Legal Name in the Appendix.

B. Notify Agencies and Institutions

In this section, we discuss how to get your name changed in business and government records. This is often the most time-consuming and frustrating part of changing your name—especially for those who are changing their name by Usage. The process involves contacting each business or agency, sometimes in person, and telling them to change your name in their records. We hope the advice we offer here will make the process as smooth as possible.

1. Court Petition and Other Court Order

For people who have a court decree documenting their name change, we recommend you first obtain a Social Security card in your new name. Then, acquire a driver's license or DMV-issued ID card. (See Section B3, below, for detailed instructions on having your name changed on these or other records.)

Once you have these two pieces of identification in your new name, it should be no problem having your other records changed.

You must get a new Social Security card *before* going to the DMV. In an effort to curb identity theft, the DMV will not issue a license (or a renewal) unless the name precisely matches the name on your Social Security card.

2. Usage Method

Letting everyone know about your name change is particularly important with a Usage method change. Obviously, it will be difficult for you to use your new name if all of your identification and records list your old name. Unfortunately, convincing some government agencies to change your name without a court order will be no easy task. Once you get a few official documents with your new name, however, it will become easier to get more and eventually to have your name completely accepted.

As described in Chapter 1, despite the fact that Usage method name changes are legal, there is a trend for government agencies to resist name changes without a court order, except in the case of marriage. The DMV is most restrictive, making it impossible to get a driver's license in your new name unless you have first obtained a new Social Security card (even if you have a marriage license or a court decree, the DMV will not change your name unless you can produce a new Social Security card).

The Social Security Administration and the U.S. State Department, which issue Social Security cards and passports, accept a variety of documentation to show a name change. This includes IDs issued by schools, health insurance companies and employers. For this reason, we recommend proceeding along the following order in your Usage method record-changing process.

- Start with your employer and/or school. Tell them you have changed your name and request a new ID card or other document list-

DECLARATION OF LEGAL NAME CHANGE

I, the undersigned, declare that I am 18 years of age or older and further declare:

1. I, _____**[name presently used]**_____, was born _____**[name on birth certificate]**_____ in _____**[county where born]**_ County in the State of ___**[state where born]**_____ on **[birthdate, year]**_____.

2. I HEREBY DECLARE my intent to change my legal name, and be henceforth exclusively known as _____**[new name]**_____.

3. I further declare that I have no intention of defrauding any person or escaping any obligation I may presently have by this act.

4. NOTICE IS HEREBY GIVEN to all agencies of the State of California, all agencies of the Federal Government, all creditors and all private persons, groups, businesses, corporations and associations of said legal name change.

I declare under penalty of perjury under the laws of the State of California that the foregoing is true and correct.

Dated: _____   _____
                                                                      (new signature)

                                               _____
                                                                      (old signature)

NOTARIZATION

State of California
County of _____ } ss

On this _____ day of _____, _____, before me, _____
_____, a notary public of the State of California, personally
appeared _____, personally known to me (or proved
to me on the basis of satisfactory evidence) to be the person(s) whose name(s) is/are subscribed to the within instrument, and acknowledged to me that she/he/they executed the same in her/his/their authorized capacities, and that by her/his/their signature(s) on the instrument the person(s), or the entity upon behalf of which the person(s) acted, executed the instrument.

WITNESS my hand and official seal. _____
                                                                Signature of Notary Public

[Notary Seal]   Notary Public for the State of California

                                       My commission expires: _____, _____

DECLARATION RESTORING FORMER LEGAL NAME

I, the undersigned, declare that I am 18 years of age or older and further declare:

1. The name I am presently using is _____ **[name presently used]** _____ .

2. My marital status is as follows *(optional):*

    a. ❑ I was legally divorced in the State of _____ **[state in which divorce occurred]** _____ on

    [date of decree, including year]

    b. ❑ My marriage was legally annulled in the State of _**[state in which annulment occurred]**_ on

    **[date of decree, including year]**

    c. ❑ I am legally married.

    d. ❑ I am single.

3. I HEREBY DECLARE my intent to return to my former legal name, and be henceforth exclusively known

as _____ **[former legal name]** _____ .

4. I have no intention of defrauding any person or escaping any obligation I may presently have by this act.

5. NOTICE IS HEREBY GIVEN to all agencies of the State of California, all agencies of the Federal Government, all creditors and all private persons, groups, businesses, corporations and associations of said legal name change.

I declare under penalty of perjury under the laws of the State of California that the foregoing is true and correct.

Dated: _____

_____
(new signature)

_____
(old signature)

NOTARIZATION

State of California

County of _____ } ss

On this _____ day of _____, _____ , before me, _____ , a notary public of the State of California, personally appeared _____ , personally known to me (or proved to me on the basis of satisfactory evidence) to be the person(s) whose name(s) is/are subscribed to the within instrument, and acknowledged to me that she/he/they executed the same in her/his/their authorized capacity(ies), and that by her/his/their signature(s) on the instrument the person(s), or the entity upon behalf of which the person(s) acted, executed the instrument.

WITNESS my hand and official seal. _____

Signature of Notary Public

[Notary Seal]

Notary Public for the State of California

My commission expires: _____ , _____

ing your new name. Especially if you work for a small employer, this may be easy.

- Ask your insurers to change your name in their records and issue you a new ID card.
- Ask your banks, lenders, credit card companies and other financial companies you deal with to change your name in their records.
- Apply for a new passport, using these pieces of identification. This should be sufficient to get your new name on your passport. But if you have been using your new name for less than five years (or if you are unable to prove that you have been using your name for five years), your new passport will list your old name plus your new name as an AKA (also known as).
- Use the passport and new ID cards to have a new Social Security card issued.
- Apply to the DMV for a new driver's license or California ID card, using your new Social Security card as proof of your change.

We realize that this sounds like a lot of work. But, having your name changed in all of these records just doesn't happen by itself. Even if you went to court and had your name officially changed, you would still have to contact all these agencies (but it would be easier at each step along the way).

⚠ Getting Usage method name changes accepted can be tricky. We can't promise that the approach we suggest above will work to get a new name established by the Usage method. That, of course, is the big reason why throughout this book we recommend the Court Petition method. But if you attempt a Usage method name change and you're having problems getting your

usage name change accepted, it may work to shuffle the paperwork process a bit. For instance, if your school is fussy about changing your name, you might try using your bank account or insurance ID card to get a Social Security card or passport; then use one of these to get your school to accept your change.

If you run into an uncooperative clerk, ask to speak to his supervisor. You also may want to gently but forcefully give the person a rundown of California law: Politely explain that California adults have the right to change their names without going to court. Keep going up the ladder until you get results. If you have trouble at the local office of a government agency, contact the main office. You can even try enlisting the help of a local elected official. We have written up a short summary of California name-change law. You can try showing a copy to bureaucrats who refuse to change their records. We hope it helps!

▤ A tear-out version of "Changing Your Name by the Usage Method" is in the Appendix. You can make copies to show reluctant bureaucrats who might doubt your right to change your name by the Usage method.

Changing Your Name by the Usage Method

In California, adults can legally change their names in two ways, either by filing a court petition or by consistently using their new name for all business purposes without going to court. California's legislature and courts have long recognized the right of adults to change their names without petitioning a court. For example, the most respected legal treatise relied on by judges, lawyers and law students, *Summary of California Law* (Witkin), states, "A person has a common law right to change his name without applying to a court." Witkin, 4 *Summary of Cal. L.*, Ch. VIII, § 16 (9th ed. 1987).

True, the California legislature has also created a process by which a person *may* go to court to change his name. Described in Civil Procedure Code Sections 1275 to 1279.6, this process is designed to record a person's change. None of these laws alter the fact that California courts have repeatedly stated that changing your name by consistently using a new name is legal:

"A person may change his name at any time without initiating legal proceedings." *In re Marriage of Banks*, 42 Cal. App. 3d 631 (1974).

"The common law recognizes a right of a person to change his name without the necessity of legal proceedings; the purpose of the statutory procedure is simply to have, wherever possible, the change recorded." *In re Ritchie*, 159 Cal. App. 3d 1070 (1984).

An adult "has a common law right to change his name ... without the necessity of any legal proceeding." *Lee v. Ventura County Superior Court*, 9 Cal. App. 4th 510 (1992).

Since Californians clearly have the legal right to change their names by consistently using a new name in place of an old one, private businesses and governmental agencies should be willing to change all records reflecting a person's name upon request.

3. How to Change Identification and Records—A Chart

Agencies and businesses have varying requirements before they will issue new identification for you or change you name in their records. The following chart tells you what the most commonly used agencies require as of 2001. If you changed your name by obtaining a court order, including those issued as part of a divorce or adoption, follow the chart's instructions for the Court Petition method rather than the Usage method. Also, if you changed your name at marriage, follow the Court Petition method.

Most agencies and businesses will want to see certified copies of all court orders and other key legal documents. However, if you changed your name on getting married, you do not need to provide a certified copy of your marriage license. A photocopy of your original should work.

	COURT PETITION	**USAGE METHOD**
Social Security	To obtain a Social Security card in your new name, file an Application for a Social Security Card (Form SS-5). These forms are available on the Social Security Administration's website, http://www.ssa.gov, at your local Social Security office or by calling 800-772-1213. There is no charge. • driver's license If you already have a Social Security number, use this form to change your name (don't request a new Social Security number). Attach a certified copy of your Decree or other court order. You will probably need to show one additional piece of identification. Acceptable forms of identification are listed in the Usage method column at the right. If you are applying for a Social Security number for the first time, you'll also need a certified copy of your birth certificate.	Same as Court Petition, but instead of the court order, you'll need to present one ID which lists both names or two pieces of identification: one in your old name and one in your new name. Acceptable forms of identification include original or certified copies of your: • employer ID card • passport • school ID card, record or report card • marriage, divorce or adoption records • health insurance card • military records, or • insurance policy. They may also accept other documents that include enough information to identify you.
Driver's License or California ID Card	Go to the local Department of Motor Vehicles and fill out a Form DL-44. Check the box on the form entitled "Name Change." In addition to a new Social Security card, you will need to provide one of the following forms of evidence of your new name: • a government-issued document containing your name, date of birth and, if available, a government seal, such as an adoption or divorce order, marriage certificate or name change decree • birth certificate • military ID, or • passport. However, it is not presently clear whether the DMV will accept a passport as proof of your new name if it still lists your old name with your new name listed after AKA (also known as). You will need to surrender your current license or ID card and pay the required fee. You will also have to be photographed and give a thumbprint. If you do not currently have a driver's license or ID card, you'll need to bring along an original or certified copy of your birth certificate, even though your new name will differ from the one on your birth certificate, plus your new Social Security card. If you weren't born in the U.S., you'll also need proof that you're legally in the country, such as a green card or naturalization papers (Cal. Veh. Code § 12801.5). Information is available at the DMV website, http://www.dmv.ca.gov; however the Form DL-44 is not currently available on the site.	Same as Court Petition. But following the instructions in Section B, above, be sure you have acquired a Social Security card in your new name before attempting to change your name at the DMV.

	COURT PETITION	**USAGE METHOD**
Federal Income Tax	Make arrangements at work for your paychecks, withholding and W-2 forms to be in your new name. The SS-5 form filled out for Social Security is automatically forwarded to the Internal Revenue Service, so you are not required to separately contact the IRS about your name change. Simply file your next income tax return using your new name and old Social Security number. (You may file in your new name even if your W-2 is still in your old name, but of course you'll also want to have your employer make the change.) A married couple can file a joint income tax form using two different names. Just write your new name(s) on the form. There is space on the tax forms for each spouse's last name.	Same as Court Petition.
State Income Tax	Send a letter to Taxpayer Services, Franchise Tax Board, P.O. Box 942840, Sacramento, California 94240-5340. Say that you have changed your name and give your old name, new name and Social Security number. Use your new name and old Social Security number when filing any later tax returns or forms.	Same as Court Petition.
Voting	Register under your new name by completing an Affidavit of Voter Registration, available by contacting the Registrar of Voters. If you have been registered to vote before, you will need to state the name, address and political party listed in your most recent registration. Take or mail the completed form to the county Registrar of Voters. Once you've registered, you can vote and sign petitions using your new name.	Same as Court Petition.
Passports	With a court order or marriage certificate, you have two choices: **Amend Passport.** You can have your current passport amended to reflect both your old and new names. The passport office simply adds a piece of paper to the back of your passport, listing your new name. Use "Passport Amendment/Validation Application" (Form DSP-19). There is no charge, and you can send in the application by mail. **Obtain New Passport.** You can get a new passport that shows only your new name. If you have been issued a U.S. passport within the last 15 years or it has been less than five years since your passport expired, you can apply by mail and pay a $40 fee using "Application for Passport by Mail" (Form DSP-82). If you have not been issued a U.S. passport within the last 15 years, you must apply in person. Use "Application for Passport" (Form DSP-11) and pay the $60 fee. In addition to your proof of name change, you must provide proof of citizenship, such as a certified copy of your birth certificate and a piece of identification with your new name and signature—such as a driver's license or photo ID from your work, the military or U.S. government.	If you can show that you have been using your new name for five years OR one of the following exceptions applies: • the new name is similar to the old—for example, the name change consists of transposing first and middle names, making minor spelling changes, adding or deleting a first or middle name, adopting a common nickname or Americanizing a foreign first or middle name • you are a married, divorced or widowed woman using your birth or previous married name exclusively, or • your name was not recorded at birth, was recorded incorrectly or was changed during childhood. then you have a choice. Obtain New Passport, or Amend Passport. You can obtain a passport exclusively in your new name or have your current passport amended to show you changed your name. Use the forms and rules that are listed in the Court Petition column. You will also have to provide five public documents that show you have used your name for five years. In place

	COURT PETITION	**USAGE METHOD**
Passports (continued)	For information and forms, see the State Department's Passport Services website at http://travel.state.gov/passport_services.html. You can also obtain copies of applications by contacting an office that handles passports, such as post offices or county clerk's offices. Or contact: Los Angeles Passport Agency Federal Building, Suite 1000 11000 Wilshire Boulevard Los Angeles, CA 90024-3615 San Francisco Passport Agency 95 Hawthorne Street, 5th Floor San Francisco, CA 94105-3901	of one public document, you can provide two affidavits from friends or relatives who know about the change. Acceptable documents include: • tax documents • school records or ID • credit card or statement • insurance records or ID • voter registration • utility bills • lease or mortgage • employment ID or records, including payment stub • bank statement • Social Security card • property tax assessment • vehicle registration or title, or • military documents. If you cannot show you have used your name for five years and one of the above exceptions does not apply, your only option is to obtain a new passport, which lists your old name plus your new name as an AKA (also known as). Apply in person with the "Application for Passport" (Form DSP-11). Follow the instructions in the Court Petition column and also provide three public documents showing your new name. **Children's Names.** If a child is known by her stepfather's last name, a passport may sometimes be issued in that name, even though a legal adoption has not taken place. This requires the written consent of the natural father or a special affidavit by the mother indicating that the natural father is dead or his whereabouts are unknown.
Bank Accounts	Go to your bank in person and tell them you've changed your name. Provide a certified copy of the Decree or other court order. Most banks will also insist on seeing some piece of identification with your new name and photo, such as a driver's license. You will need to sign a new signature card, and probably re-do all prior documentation to reflect your name change. For a while, banks will probably cross-list you in their records under both your new and old names. But if you expect to receive checks made payable to your old name, advise the bank officer and make sure this is done. Remember to order checks with your new name.	Same as Court Petition, with the exception that you will not provide a copy of the court order. Bring what you have in your new name with you.
Credit Cards	Notify your credit card companies of the change and request new cards. To protect your credit history, make sure that the original date of the account is included along with your new name.	Same as Court Petition.

	COURT PETITION	**USAGE METHOD**
Credit Cards (continued)	**Women's Names** California law provides that no business may refuse to do business with a woman because she uses her birth or former name, regardless of her marital status (Cal. Civ. Proc. Code § 1279.6). Credit card companies are required by law to issue credit cards in a woman's birth or married name—the choice of name is entirely up to her. However, the credit card company may insist that a married woman establish an account separate from her husband's (Cal. Civ. Code § 1747.81). If you have previously been known by your married name, your credit records may be in your husband's name only and may not reflect your credit history. To ensure that you have a credit history in your own name, write to your credit card company and make sure it reports your new name with the original opening date of the joint account.	
Public Assistance (Welfare)	Take a certified copy of the Decree or court order to your local welfare office. The office will change its records so you will receive payments under your new name. When you complete your monthly reporting statement, indicate that you have changed your name. You can fill in the information in the section that asks whether you have anything else to report.	Same as Court Petition, but simply tell the local welfare office you have changed your name and give your new name.
Birth Certificates and Attachments	Information on California birth certificates and details about when they can be amended or reissued is covered in Chapter 5. If you were born outside of California, check with the vital statistics office in the state or country of your birth. If you changed your name by court petition, you can have an amendment attached to your birth certificate reflecting your new name. Usage method, the state will add an official attachment reflecting the parent's new name to the child's birth certificate. See Chapter 5, Section A.	You cannot receive a new California birth certificate or amend your birth certificate by adding an official attachment based on a name change without a court order. See Chapter 5 for more information on when you can obtain a new or amended birth certificate. However, if a parent changes her name by the
Stocks, Bonds, Mutual Funds, Retirement Accounts	If you actually have possession of the stock or bond certificate, you will probably need to send it along with a signed letter to the transfer agent listed on the certificate. But it's best to call first and see what their exact rules are. Assuming you send a certificate by mail, make a photocopy in case the original is lost. You will receive a certificate in your new name. If, as is more likely, your stock is held in one or more brokerage accounts (you don't have physical possession of the certificates), call the broker to learn procedures for charging the account. This will normally involve sending them a copy of your certified court decree.	Same as Court Petition.

	COURT PETITION	**USAGE METHOD**
Autos, Boats and Planes	**Autos and Boats:** To have a vehicle reregistered in your new name, go to the Department of Motor Vehicles. Complete a "Statement of Facts" (Form REG-256), and file it with your existing title (pink slip) to have a new Certificate of Title issued. To change the title, you must be the full legal owner. Or you must contact the institution that holds the title and request that it initiate the name change. This usually isn't necessary until you're ready to sell the vehicle. **Planes:** To change your name on your plane's registration, you'll need to get a Form AC 8050-2 from the FAA's Flight Standards District Office in your area. You can find the FSDO closest to you in the government pages of the phone book. You'll need to fill out the form with your new name and send it along with a $5 fee and a bill of sale or proof of ownership to: FAA Aircraft Registry, Mike Monroney Aeronautical Center, P.O. Box 25504, Oklahoma City OK 73125.	Same as Court Petition.
Deeds to Real Estate	If you own real estate, you should change the deed to reflect your new name. This will avoid confusion if you sell or refinance your property. It also will show you did not change your name with the intent of defrauding anyone. You must list both your former and new names on the deed when you sell your property (Cal. Civ. Code §1096). Here is how to change your deed. Go to a stationery store or a title company and pick up a blank deed that corresponds to your deed (usually a "grant" deed). Or use a copy from *The Deeds Book: How to Transfer Title to California Real Estate*, by Mary Randolph (Nolo). Draw up a new deed following the basic form of your old deed but transferring the property from your former name to your new name. Use wording such as: "[New Name], who acquired title under the former name of [Former Name], hereby grants to [New Name] the following property:" Then include the full legal description of the property. Above the main part of the deed, there will be a section on transfer tax. If available, check the box before words such as, "This transfer is exempt from the documentary transfer tax." Or type in the words, "no valuable consideration." Sign the deed in your new name and have it notarized. Complete a Preliminary Change of Ownership Report, available from the county recorder or county assessor. Where the form requires transfer information, indicate that the transaction is only a correction of the name on the deed.	Same as Court Petition.

	COURT PETITION	**USAGE METHOD**
Deeds to Real Estate (continued)	Finally, record your deed with the county recorder's office and pay the small fee. In some courts, you will have to pay an additional fee for file-stamped copies.	
Mortgages	Notify the mortgage company of your new name. There is no change in your liability for the mortgage.	Same as Court Petition.
Wills, Estate Planning and Inheritances	**Your Will** If you have made a will or other estate planning documents, such as a living trust, it is best to avoid confusion by replacing them with new documents reflecting your new name. It's probably best to revise your will anyway, but should you fail to do this, your relatives will not lose their inheritances just because you change your name. **Someone Else's Will** Don't worry—you won't lose your inheritance by changing your name, even if you are listed in someone's will in your old name. As long as you are the person listed in the will, it makes no difference that your name is different. For example, a woman who changes her name by marriage does not lose any inheritance listed in her birth name. To avoid any confusion, when someone dies who might have left you an inheritance, notify the executor or administrator of the estate of your old and new names.	Same as Court Petition.
Insurance	Let your insurance carrier know of your name change. Have policies reissued in your new name. They may request a copy of your court order—be prepared to send them one. **Automobile Insurance:** Notify your agent of the name change. Auto insurance rates are not affected by name changes. **Health Insurance:** Notify the insurance carrier of the change. If you have coverage through your spouse's employer, your spouse may have to sign a form requesting that a card be issued in your new name under the same coverage. **Life Insurance:** Notify the company of the name change if you hold a policy or are the beneficiary of a policy. Should you neglect to notify a company of the name change, it won't alter your right to receive insurance proceeds.	Same as Court Petition.
Creditors and Debtors	Changing your name obviously does not make your debts disappear. Notify your creditors about the change, including holders of promissory notes, medical and legal professionals, landlords and anyone who obtained a court judgment against you.	Same as Court Petition.

	COURT PETITION	**USAGE METHOD**
Creditors and Debtors (continued)	You'll need to contact anyone who owes you money, such as renters or debtors against whom you obtained a court judgment. Notify them of your new name and ask that payments be made in your new name. Changing your name does not affect their debt to you.	
Post Office	List both your old and new name on your mailbox, so the carrier will know to deliver mail addressed to you in either name. Eventually, you should receive all mail in your new name and may then want to remove your old name from the mailbox.	Same as Court Petition.
Telephone and Utilities	Contact the telephone company and advise it of the name change. If you want to be listed in the directory under both old and new names, there will be a small monthly charge. Or, more likely, you could arrange to be listed only in your new name. Contact your local utility companies and advise them of the name change. If you change both your first and last names, you may have problems with local utilities, especially if they require a deposit for new customers. Let them know you've changed your name but are the same person and can provide them with documentation to that effect. You may then need to send a copy of the Decree or other court order.	Same as Court Petition, but if documentation is required, you can use a name change declaration presented in Section A, above.
School Records	Have your schools change your name on their records in case an employer sends for copies of your grades. (Sunday schools are optional.) You can also petition the school to have your diploma reissued in your new name.	Same as Court Petition.
Veterans Administration	Contact the local VA office and let it know you have changed your name. Some offices will accept a letter signed in your new name. Or you can fill in Form 21-4138, a blank form put out by the VA. Including a certified copy of the Decree or other court order may be helpful.	Same as Court Petition, but if documentation is required, you can use a name change declaration presented in Section A, above.
Employer's Records	Let your employer know you want to be called only by your new name. Have your name changed in your employment records, including payroll and tax records. If you work as an independent contractor, give your customers your new name.	Same as Court Petition.
Legal and Other Important Documents	All important papers should be revised to reflect your new name. This includes legal documents such as durable or regular powers of attorney, living wills, trusts and contracts.	Same as Court Petition.
Other Records	Look through your correspondence, address book, the contents of your wallet and your important papers to discover if there are other people, businesses or agencies you must contact. Write a short letter stating that you have legally changed your name and want only your new name to be used from now on. No documentation is needed.	Same as Court Petition.

Finding Additional Help

Most name changes are so simple the average Joe can transform himself into the average Darren all by himself. However, if your situation turns out to be one of the very rare legally complicated name changes, you may want to do some more research or in some situations hire a lawyer.

Even if your name change appears be routine and uncomplicated, you might want someone else to type up the forms for you. (But don't forget neat hand printing is also an option in most courts.) This is normally easy to accomplish by hiring a nonlawyer legal document preparer (see Section C, below).

Finally, you may want to read up on your right to change your name without going to court, or otherwise research the subject of names and name changes. This chapter will be your first step in each of these directions.

A. When You Might Need a Lawyer

Most name changes are straightforward: An adult asks the court to change his name, the court recognizes the adult's right to go by the name of his choosing and grants the name change (usually without the need for a court appearance). The two most common situations in which a petition is more complicated are where someone objects to your name change and/or you are petitioning on behalf of a child.

Most name changes do not require the help of a lawyer. If you are petitioning for a new name on behalf of yourself and can't see someone objecting—you really shouldn't need to hire an attorney.

It is rare to have objections to an adult's name change. As we've seen in this book, though, it can happen. For example, a creditor may think you're trying to avoid payment or someone who already bears your new name may fear you're planning to use the name for fraudulent purposes. In these situations, you might want an attorney to assist you at the hearing. However, if you have a good handle on your reasons for changing your name and if your opponent's arguments seem easy to refute, you should be able to handle the hearing on your own. And you can save a few dollars by completing the forms yourself.

Changing a child's name is often more complicated than changing an adult's. Usually, no one has an interest in an adult's name besides the adult herself. On the other hand, many people may have an interest in a child's name; the parents, a legal guardian, other relatives, the child himself and the court could have an opinion and the right to have that opinion heard. And because more people are typically involved, the chances of someone objecting are greater. Common situations in which someone disputes a child's proposed name change include:

- You are a recently divorced mother with joint custody of your two daughters. Your daughters are with you five nights per week. You have returned to your birth name and want your little girls to share your last name. Your ex believes that it's at best premature to change the children's names.

- You share 50/50 custody of your son with your ex-husband. You have been divorced five years and you're both very active in your child's life. You were remarried a year ago and took your new husband's name. You're pregnant again and plan to give your new child your new husband's name. You want your son to share the last name of the rest of your family. However, your former husband believes just as strongly that his son should retain his name, and your son is conflicted about the proposed change.

- You became legal guardian of your close friends' daughter when your friends were tragically killed two years ago. Your new daughter sees a lot of her biological grandparents, but she is now firmly rooted in your nuclear family. You think it would be best for her to share her new family's name, but her grandparents aren't so sure.

In situations like these, it may make sense to hire an attorney. Assuming the person who has doubts about the name change goes to court to oppose it, these cases will require you to convince the court that a change is in the child's best interests (see Chapters 4 and 6 for more on children's name changes). An attorney will be able to fashion arguments, research similar cases and deal with the other side's attorney. Of course, these are things you could do yourself, but you may conclude that it's worth the cost to hire an expert.

Name change petitions for children can occasionally be problematic even when there are no objections. For instance, you may not know where the child's other parent is, or you may have a strong reason for not wanting to inform the other parent, who has threatened you or the children. In these cases, you might want an attorney to handle only part of the case; for example, the attorney could prepare your application to the court to waive the notice requirement. If you trust yourself to put your arguments down on paper in a clear manner, however, you can handle the other paperwork on your own.

B. Hiring an Attorney

Finding a knowledgeable lawyer you trust and who charges reasonable prices is not always an easy task. It is natural to feel a little intimidated, but try to remember that a lawyer is simply a service provider you hire to do specific tasks for you. He will not take over your fundamental decision-making. Here are some suggestions for finding and hiring lawyers. You may need to look around for a bit before you find someone you feel comfortable hiring.

1. Know What You Want Your Lawyer to Do

Before you contact a lawyer, you must decide what you want the lawyer to do. Do you want to hand the entire case over to the lawyer? Or do you want him to do only a part of the case, such as representing you at the court hearing or making a particular application to the court? Your answer to these questions will depend on how complicated the case is.

In the previous section, we discussed a number of different times in which you might want a lawyer to help you with your name change petition. In each of these, though, you might need the lawyer to do different things.

- If you are changing your own name and believe someone may object, you might be able to do your own paperwork but arrange for help at the hearing.
- If you are petitioning on behalf of a child and expect objections, you might want an attorney to handle your entire case.
- If you are petitioning on behalf of a child and can't find or don't want to notify the other parent, you might want an attorney to handle your application to waive notice.

2. Finding a Lawyer

The first thing you should know as you start your attorney search is that few lawyers have a lot of experience with name change petitions. That's because petitioning a court to change a name is such a simple procedure, loads of people do it themselves. The result is that many lawyers in general practice may not know as much about the details of the procedure as is contained in this book. Family lawyers who handle divorce, adoptions and guardianships are most likely to be conversant with name change law, especially as it relates to changing the names women and children.

a.   Talk to Your Friends and Colleagues

One good way to find a lawyer is through a referral from a satisfied and knowledgeable customer. People who have been through a divorce or a custody dispute may be able to supply you with the name of a good family lawyer. If you can only find a referral for an excellent general practice lawyer (or even a lawyer with a different specialty), try calling that lawyer for a recommendation for a family lawyer.

b.   Attorney Referral Services

A lawyer referral service will give you the name of an attorney who practices in your area and handles family law issues. Most county bar associations operate these services, which you can find listed in the phone book. If you are lucky, you will receive a referral to a competent, experienced person.

Unfortunately, few lawyer referral services meaningfully screen the attorneys they list, which means those lawyers who participate may not be the most experienced or competent available. Sometimes the lawyers who sign up with referral services are just starting out and need clients. In other instances, they are people who have been practicing for years, but want more clients. Be sure to take the time to check out the credentials and experience of the person to whom you're referred.

c.   The Martindale-Hubbell Law Directory

The Martindale-Hubbell Law Directory is big, multi-volume guide which lists most United States lawyers. You can find the complete set in a law library or online at http://www.martindale.com. You can look up lawyers by name, location and specialty. Probably the best use of the directory is to find out more about the lawyers whom friends and associates recommend.

d.   The Yellow Pages and the Internet

Every phone book in America is dripping with ads for attorneys. And, of course, many websites also try to match lawyers and potential clients. Choosing a lawyer from these lists is normally not your best choice. That's because these sources basically list all lawyers who have paid for the publicity. Although some websites claim to screen lawyers, this usually consists of little more than checking to see that they are accredited to practice and possibly that a couple of personal or professional references check out.

e.   Legal Advice Without Representation

Nolo's website, http://www.nolo.com, features an Ask an Attorney service provided by lawyers associated with ARAG, a large prepaid legal insurer. For $39.95, you can discuss your name change or other legal problem with a California lawyer. If you are dissatisfied with the information or advice you receive, you can take advantage of ARAG's money-back guarantee.

3.   Dealing With a Lawyer

As we mention above, you should decide what kind of help you really need before you talk to a lawyer. For example, if you don't make it clear you want limited help, you may find yourself agreeing to turn over your entire name change process at a hefty fee.

Lawyer fees usually range from $150 to $350 or more per hour. But price is not always related to quality. It depends on the area of the county you live in, but generally, fees of $150 to $200 per hour are the norm in urban areas. In rural areas and smaller cities, $100 to $150 is more like it. It is also common for lawyers to quote fixed fees for simple legal actions, such as a name change. For example, a lawyer might agree to handle an adult's name change for $500, $750 or $1,000.

Be sure you settle your fee arrangement—preferably in writing—at the start of your relationship. In addition, you should get a clear, written commitment from the lawyer about the extent of the work he will handle. For example, if you suspect your petition to change a child's name is likely to be contested, you can ask the lawyer to quote you a firm fixed fee, no matter how many hours the procedure takes.

C. Legal Document Assistants ("Typing Services")

Until recently, if you didn't hire a lawyer to help with a legal problem, you had two choices: You could handle the problem on your own or not handle it at all. Now, a number of businesses known variously as "legal document assistants," "paralegals," "legal typing services" or "independent paralegals" have emerged to assist people in filling out legal forms. Simple procedures such as name changes, uncontested divorces and bankruptcies are all routinely handled by these nonlawyer legal document preparation services at a substantially lower cost than lawyers would charge.

These companies are very different from lawyers, since they can't give legal advice or represent you in court. They can, however,

- provide instructions and legal information needed to handle your own name change
- provide the appropriate forms, and
- type your papers so they'll be accepted by a court.

As a general matter, the longer a typing service has been in business, the better. People at the company should be up front with you about not being attorneys and not providing legal advice. A recommendation from someone who has used a particular typing service is the best way to find a reputable one in your area. The services often advertise in classified sections of local newspapers. They may be listed in the Yellow Pages under "typing services," "legal services," "paralegals" or "legal docu-

ment assistants." In addition, this book lists a number of legal document assistants and tells you how long they have prepared name change petitions. Nolo has charged an advertising fee for these listings.

D. Doing Your Own Legal Research

Legal research is how you learn about the law. It is not a skill reserved exclusively for lawyers; you can find the answers to your legal questions if you are armed with a little bit of patience and a good road map. The best legal research method depends on what you need to find out.

Fortunately, the law governing name changes is not particularly difficult to research. You probably won't need to go beyond some California laws (statutes) and, in some instances, court cases interpreting these laws. But first, you'll need a law library or a computer with online access.

1. Going to the Law Library

Every California county maintains a law library that is required to serve all members of the public—not just lawyers and judges. Although some libraries have more books than others, all have the California statutes, written court opinions and expert commentary. In addition, some larger public libraries have extensive collections of law and legal research books. Before making a special trip to the law library, you may first want to check with your main branch public library.

When you get to the library, you'll probably need the help of a good legal research guidebook (see "Legal Research: How to Find and Understand the Law," below) and a kind reference librarian. Thankfully, law librarians are almost always helpful and courteous to non-lawyers who try to do their own legal research.

a. Looking Up Statutes

State statutes are laws passed by the state legislature. This book includes many numbered references to California statutes. California's statutes are organized by topic, such as the Civil Code, Code of Civil Procedure, Family Code and Health and Safety Code. Most laws having to do with name changes are in the Code of Civil Procedure.

Every law library and some regular public libraries will have copies of these California codes. You can also find the statutes online. One easy place to find them is through Nolo's website (http://www.nolo.com). In the middle of Nolo's home page under the Free Legal Information and Tools area, you'll see a link to Nolo's Legal Research Center. Click on State Laws and you'll find a link to California's statutes.

When you look for statutes (also called the state code) at the library, you'll find them in two versions: books, containing only the laws themselves, and books with annotated codes. The annotated version, which is not available for free online, can be helpful when dealing with more complicated legal issues, because it includes summaries of court opinions (cases) interpreting the law and other resources following the text of each law. But the case law summaries are just that, so read the full text of the court decision yourself rather than just relying on the summary.

b. Looking Up Cases

"Case law" refers to a court's written opinion, resolving one or more issues of a particular lawsuit. Court opinions, also called cases, do one of two things. First, courts interpret statutes, regulations and ordinances so that we know how they apply in real-life situations. Second, courts make rules that are not found in statutes, regulations or ordinances. Often these decisions are in areas not clearly covered by a statute. These court-made laws are called the "common law."

The right to change your name without going to court is a common law right. It was created by the courts rather than the legislature. This means that none of the state statutes say specifically that you can change your name without going to court. But a number of cases say just this, including *In re Marriage of Banks*, 42 Cal. App. 3d 631 (1974), which states, "A person may change his name at any time without initiating legal proceedings." To learn about your right to change your name without going to court, you'll have to read cases, such as *Banks*. If you can find a case with facts similar to your situation, you can get some guidance on how a court might decide your case.

California Courts Approve the Usage Method

If you wish to do more research on your right to change your name via the Usage method, check out the following California court decisions: *Lee v. Ventura County Superior Court*, 9 Cal. App. 4th 510, 513, 11 Cal. Rptr. 2d 763 (1992); *Cabrera v. McMullen*, 204 Cal. App. 3d 1 (1988); *In re Ritchie*, 159 Cal. App. 3d 1070 (1984); *In re Banks Marriage*, 42 Cal. App. 3d 631 (1974); *Sousa v. Freitas*, 10 Cal. App. 3d 660 (1970); *Application of Trower*, 260 Cal. App. 2d 75 (1968). All basically state that that the court procedure for changing one's name does not affect the right of California adults to change their names without going to court.

California cases are published in four different sets of books: California Reports ("Cal.") covers cases from the California Supreme Court; California Appellate Reports ("Cal. App.") publishes appellate court cases; California Reporter ("Cal. Rptr.") includes both Supreme and appellate court cases; and the Pacific Reporter ("P.") publishes Supreme and pre-1960 appellate court cases, along with cases from the other Western states.

A "case citation" is a shorthand identification of the volume, series of reporter and page number where the case can be found. Or put another way, a citation is a case's address: It tells you where to find it. Take as an example, the *Banks* case, listed above. Its citation is 42 Cal. App. 3d 631 (1974); this tells you it is in Volume 42 of California Appellate Reports (third series) on page 631. Each citation has the same format: volume, reporter (including series) and page. One case can have a few different citations, since it may be listed in a few different reporters. The citation will list the reporter by the abbreviation listed in parentheses after each reporter's name, above.

You can also find many California cases online. One of the best websites for researching case law is FindLaw (http://www.findlaw.com). At the time of this printing, you can find the cases listed above free of charge, though you will have to register with the website.

Legal Research: How to Find and Understand the Law, by Stephen Elias and Susan Levinkind (Nolo), is a hands-on guide to the law library, including online resources. It addresses research methods in detail and should answer most questions that arise in the course of your research. It also contains a good discussion of how to read and analyze statutes.

2. Online Legal Research

Another way to approach legal research is to use a computer. If you want the text of a California statute, information about a recent court decision or a copy of a legal form, you'll probably be able to find it on the Internet.

You may want to start by visiting Nolo's site at http://www.nolo.com. We offer extensive material on a wide variety of legal subjects, including more information about doing your own legal research, on paper and online. We also have links to California statutes and to county courthouses across California. You can use this feature to find a copy of your local Superior Court's local rules. As we mention in Chapter 6, local rules govern particulars like which branch court you should file with (if your court has branches) and the exact form your papers should be in for the court to accept them. In the middle of Nolo's home page, find the Free Legal Information and Tools box. Under Court Information, click on Federal, State and Local. From here, follow links to your county and court's local rules.

Here are some other websites which can help you find:

- **Court Rules.** California Judicial Council (http://www.courtinfo.ca.gov/rules).
- **Statutes.** Legislative Council of California (http://www.leginfo.ca.gov/calaw.html).
- **Cases.** FindLaw (http://www.findlaw.com) WestLaw (http://www.westlaw.com).
- **Legal Forms.** California Judicial Council (http://www.courtinfo.ca.gov/forms). ■

This Appendix includes all of the forms you will need to complete your name change, plus a sheet of blank pleading paper and "Changing Your Name in California," our explanation of the continued viability of the Usage method, which you can show to skeptical agencies or businesses. We suggest that you make a few photocopies of each form and use one for practice. When you're sure you've done it correctly, use a fresh copy and enter the information in black ink or by typewriter.

All of the forms used in Chapters 4 and 6 are designed by the California Judicial Council, and all were current when we prepared this book (September 2001). However, the Council changes its forms from time to time. To learn whether a form has been updated, turn to the form in the Appendix and look for its number and revision date, which you'll find in the lower left-hand corner. Go to the Judicial Council's website (http://www.courtinfo.ca.gov/forms) and view the forms by number. Look for your form, select it and compare its date with the date on the form in this book. If the form on the site has a more recent date than the one in this book, download the form and use it. Do not attempt to use an old form.

Chapter 4

Ex Parte Application for Restoration of Former Name After Entry of Judgment

Chapter 6

Petition for Change of Name plus its attachment, Name and Information About the Person Whose Name Is to Be Changed
Order to Show Cause for Change of Name
Decree Changing Name
Civil Case Cover Sheet
Application for Waiver of Court Fees and Costs
Order on Application for Waiver of Court Fees and Costs
Declaration of Guardian
Decree Changing Name of Minor (by Guardian)
Proof of Service of Order to Show Cause
A piece of blank pleading paper

Chapter 7

Declaration of Legal Name Change
Declaration Restoring Former Legal Name
Changing Your Name by the Usage Method

ATTORNEY OR PARTY WITHOUT ATTORNEY *(Name and Address):*	TELEPHONE NO.:	FOR COURT USE ONLY

ATTORNEY FOR *(Name):*

SUPERIOR COURT OF CALIFORNIA, COUNTY OF

STREET ADDRESS:

MAILING ADDRESS:

CITY AND ZIP CODE:

BRANCH NAME:

MARRIAGE OF

PETITIONER:

RESPONDENT:

EX PARTE APPLICATION FOR RESTORATION OF FORMER NAME AFTER ENTRY OF JUDGMENT AND ORDER	CASE NUMBER:

APPLICATION

1. A judgment of dissolution or nullity was entered on *(date):*

2. Applicant now requests that her former name be restored. Her former name is *(specify):*

Date:

....
(TYPE OR PRINT NAME)

▶ _____
(SIGNATURE OF APPLICANT)
(USE CURRENT NAME)

ORDER

3. IT IS ORDERED that applicant's former name is restored to *(specify):*

Date: _____

☐ JUDGE OF THE SUPERIOR COURT ☐ COMMISSIONER OF THE SUPERIOR COURT

[SEAL]

CLERK'S CERTIFICATE

I certify that the foregoing is a true and correct copy of the original on file in my office.

Date: Clerk, by _____, Deputy

Form Adopted by Rule 1287.50
Judicial Council of California
1287.50 [Rev. July 1, 1994]

EX PARTE APPLICATION FOR RESTORATION OF FORMER NAME AFTER ENTRY OF JUDGMENT AND ORDER
(Family Law)

WEST GROUP
Official Publisher

Family Code, § 2080

PETITIONER OR ATTORNEY *(Name, state bar number, and address):*

FOR COURT USE ONLY

TELEPHONE NO.:　　　　　FAX NO. *(Optional):*

E-MAIL ADDRESS *(Optional):*

ATTORNEY FOR *(Name):*

SUPERIOR COURT OF CALIFORNIA, COUNTY OF

　　STREET ADDRESS:

　　MAILING ADDRESS:

　　CITY AND ZIP CODE:

　　BRANCH NAME:

PETITION OF *(Names of each petitioner):*

FOR CHANGE OF NAME

PETITION FOR CHANGE OF NAME

CASE NUMBER:

Before you complete this petition, you should read the *Instructions for Filing a Petition for Change of Name* on the reverse. You must answer all questions and check all boxes on this petition that apply to you. You must file this petition in the Superior Court of the county where the person whose name is to be changed resides.

---

1. Name of each petitioner:

2. Petitioner requests that the court decree the following name changes *(list every name that you are seeking to change):*

　　　　　　　　　Present name　　　　　　　　　　　　　　　　　Proposed name

　a. _____ changed to _____

　b. _____ changed to _____

　c. _____ changed to _____

　d. _____ changed to _____

　e. _____ changed to _____

　　☐ Continued *(if you are seeking to change additional names, you must prepare a list and attach it to this petition as Attachment 2).*

3. Petitioner requests that the court issue an order directing all interested persons to appear and show cause why this petition for change of name of the persons identified in item 2 should not be granted.

4. The number of persons under 18 years of age whose names are to be changed is *(specify):* _____.

5. If this petition requests the change of name of any person or persons under 18 years, this request is being made by
　a. ☐ both parents.
　b. ☐ mother only.
　c. ☐ father only.
　d. ☐ near relative *(name and relationship):*
　e. ☐ guardian *(name):*
　f. ☐ other *(specify):*

6. For each person whose name is to be changed, petitioner provides the following information *(you must attach a separate copy of the attachment* Name and Information About the Person Whose Name Is to Be Changed *(Form NC-110) for each person identified in item 2):*

　a. 　The number of attachments included in this petition is *(specify number):* _____

　b–f. *(Attachment page or pages)*

(Instructions on reverse)

Form Adopted for Mandatory Use
Judicial Council of California
NC-100 [Rev. July 1, 2001]

PETITION FOR CHANGE OF NAME
(Change of Name)

Code of Civil Procedure, § 1275 et seq.

1. **Where to File**

   The petition for change of name must be filed in the superior court in the county where the person whose name is to be changed presently lives.

2. **Whose Name May Be Changed**

   The petition may be used to change one's own name and, under certain circumstances, the names of others (e.g., children under 18 years of age).

3. **What Forms Are Required**

   Prepare an original and two copies of each of the following documents:

   a. *Petition for Change of Name* (Form NC-100).

   b. *Name and Information About the Person Whose Name Is to Be Changed* (Form NC-110) (attach as many copies as necessary).

   c. *Order to Show Cause for Change of Name* (Form NC-120).

   d. *Decree Changing Name* (Form NC-130 or, for guardians, Form NC-130G).

   In addition, a guardian must prepare and attach a *Declaration of Guardian* (Form NC-110G) for each child whose name is to be changed.

4. **Filing and Filing Fee**

   Prepare an original *Civil Case Cover Sheet* (Form 982.2(b)(1)). File the original petition and *Civil Case Cover Sheet* with the clerk of the court and obtain two filed-endorsed copies of the petition. A filing fee will be charged unless you qualify for a fee waiver. (If you want to apply for a fee waiver, see *Application for Waiver of Court Fees and Costs* (Form 982(a)(17)); *Information Sheet on Waiver of Court Fees and Costs* (Form 982(a)(17)(A)); and *Order on Application for Waiver of Court Fees and Costs* (Form 982(a)(I8).)

5. **Requesting a Court Hearing Date**

   You should request a date for the hearing on the *Order to Show Cause* at least six weeks in the future.

6. **Filing the Order to Show Cause**

   After the hearing date has been included and you have obtained a judge's signature on the *Order to Show Cause*, file the original order in the clerk's office and obtain filed-endorsed copies of the order.

7. **Publishing the Order to Show Cause**

   A copy of the *Order to Show Cause* must be published in a local newspaper of general circulation once a week for **at least four consecutive weeks** before the date of the hearing on the name change petition. The petitioner selects the newspaper from among those newspapers legally qualified to publish orders and notices. The newspaper used must file a Proof of Publication with the superior court before the hearing. If no newspaper of general circulation is published in the county, the court may order the *Order to Show Cause* to be posted by the clerk.

8. **Name Change for Children**

   a. If a petitioning parent is requesting the name change for a child under 18 years of age, and one of the parents, if living, does not join in consenting to the name change, the petitioning parent must have a copy of the *Order to Show* Cause or notice of the time and place of the hearing served on the non-consenting parent. Service must be made **at least 30 days prior to the hearing** under Code of Civil Procedure section 413.10, 414.10, 415.10, or 415.40.

   b. If the non-consenting parent resides in California, the order or notice must be personally served on the non-consenting parent. The petitioning parent cannot personally serve this document.

   c. If the non-consenting parent resides outside California, he or she may be served by sending a copy of the order or notice by first-class mail, postage prepaid, return receipt requested.

   d. If a petition to change the name of a child has been filed by a guardian, the guardian must (1) provide notice of the hearing to any living parent of the child by personal service at least 30 days before the hearing, or (2) if either or both parents are deceased or cannot be located, serve notice of the hearing on the child's grandparents, if living, not less than 30 days before the hearing under Code of Civil Procedure section 413.10, 414.10, 415.10, or 415.40.

   If you have served a parent or grandparent, file a copy of the completed *Proof of Service of Order to Show Cause* (Form NC-121) with the court before the hearing.

9. **Domestic Violence Confidentiality Program**

   In cases where the petitioner is a participant in the domestic violence confidentiality program, the petition for name change, the order to show cause published in the newspaper, and the decree should indicate, instead of the proposed name, that the name is confidential and on file with the Secretary of State.

10. **Court Hearing**

    Bring copies of all documents to the hearing. If the judge grants the name change petition, the judge will sign the original decree.

11. If you want to amend a birth certificate to show the name change, you should contact the following office:

    Department of Health Services
    Office of Vital Records
    304 "S" Street
    Sacramento, CA 95814

Local courts may supplement these instructions. Check with the court to determine whether supplemental information is available. For instance, the court may provide you with additional written information about what department handles name change petitions, when petitions are heard, and which newspapers may be used to publish the *Order to Show Cause*.

PETITION OF (Name of petitioner or petitioners):	CASE NUMBER:
FOR CHANGE OF NAME	

NAME AND INFORMATION ABOUT THE PERSON WHOSE NAME IS TO BE CHANGED
Attachment to *Petition for Change of Name* (Form NC-100)

Attachment _____ of _____

*(You must use a **separate** attachment for **each person** whose name is to be changed. If petitioner is a guardian of a minor, a supplemental attachment, Declaration of Guardian (Form NC-110G), must also be completed and attached for each minor whose name is to be changed.)*

6. *(Continued)* Petitioner applies for a decree to change the name of the following person:

   b. ☐ Self   ☐ Other

     (1) Present name *(specify)*:

     (2) Proposed name *(specify)*:

     (3) Born on *(date of birth)*:
       and presently ☐ under 18 years of age   ☐ over 18 years of age

     (4) Born at *(place of birth)*:

     (5) Sex: ☐ Male ☐ Female

     (6) Current residence address *(street, city, county, and zip code)*:

   c. Reason for name change *(explain)*:

   d. Relationship of the petitioner to the person whose name will be changed:

     (1) ☐ self   (4) ☐ near relative *(indicate relationship)*:

     (2) ☐ parent   (5) ☐ other *(specify)*:

     (3) ☐ guardian

   e. If the person whose name will be changed is under 18 years of age, provide the names and addresses, if known, of the following persons:

     (1) Father *(name)*:   *(address)*:

     (2) Mother *(name)*:   *(address)*:

     (3) *(Only if neither parent is living)* Near relatives *(names, relationships, and addresses)*:

   f. If the person whose name will be changed is 18 years of age or older, that person must sign the following declaration:

DECLARATION

I declare under penalty of perjury under the laws of the State of California that ☐ I am not ☐ I am   under the jurisdiction of the California Department of Corrections (in state prison or on parole) **and** ☐ I am not ☐ I am   required to register as a sex offender under Penal Code section 290.

Date:

▶

_____   _____
(TYPE OR PRINT NAME OF PERSON WHOSE NAME IS TO BE CHANGED)   (SIGNATURE OF PERSON WHOSE NAME IS TO BE CHANGED)

(If petitioner is represented by an attorney, the attorney's signature follows):
Date:

▶

_____   _____
(TYPE OR PRINT NAME)   (SIGNATURE OF ATTORNEY)

(Each petitioner must sign this petition in the space provided below or, if additional pages are attached, at the end of the last attachment.) I declare under penalty of perjury under the laws of the State of California that the information in the foregoing petition is true and correct.
Date:

▶

_____   _____
(TYPE OR PRINT NAME)   (SIGNATURE OF PETITIONER)

Date:

▶

_____   _____
(TYPE OR PRINT NAME)   (SIGNATURE OF PETITIONER)

☐ ADD ADDITIONAL SIGNATURE LINES FOR ADDITIONAL PETITIONERS   ☐ SIGNATURE OF PETITIONERS FOLLOWS LAST ATTACHMENT

Form Adopted for Mandatory Use
Judicial Council of California
NC-110 [New January 1, 2001]

**ATTACHMENT TO
PETITION FOR CHANGE OF NAME**

WEST GROUP
Official Publisher

Code of Civil Procedure, § 1275 et seq.

PETITIONER OR ATTORNEY *(Name, state bar number, and address)*:

TELEPHONE NO.:   FAX NO. *(Optional)*:

E-MAIL ADDRESS *(Optional)*:

ATTORNEY FOR *(Name)*:

SUPERIOR COURT OF CALIFORNIA, COUNTY OF

STREET ADDRESS:

MAILING ADDRESS:

CITY AND ZIP CODE:

BRANCH NAME:

PETITION OF *(Names of each petitioner)*:

FOR CHANGE OF NAME

ORDER TO SHOW CAUSE FOR CHANGE OF NAME	CASE NUMBER:

TO ALL INTERESTED PERSONS:

1. Petitioner *(name of each)*:   filed a petition with this court
for a decree changing names as follows:

Present name		Proposed name
a. _____	to	_____
b. _____	to	_____
c. _____	to	_____
d. _____	to	_____
e. _____	to	_____

☐ Continued on Attachment 1.

2. THE COURT ORDERS that all persons interested in this matter shall appear before this court at the hearing indicated below to show cause, if any, why the petition for change of name should not be granted.

NOTICE OF HEARING

a. Date: Time: ☐ Dept.:   ☐ Room:

b. The address of the court is ☐ same as noted above ☐ other *(specify)*:

3. a. ☐ A copy of this *Order to Show Cause* shall be published at least once each week for four successive weeks prior to the date set for hearing on the petition in the following newspaper of general circulation, printed in this county *(specify newspaper)*:

   b. ☐ Other *(specify)*:

Date: _____

_____
JUDGE OF THE SUPERIOR COURT

NOTE: When a *Petition for Change of Name* has been filed for a child and the other parent, if living, does not join in consenting to the name change, the petitioner must have a notice of the time and place of the hearing or a copy of the *Order to Show Cause* served on the other parent not less than 30 days prior to the hearing under Code of Civil Procedure section 413.10, 414.10, 415.10, or 415.40. If a petition to change the name of a child has been filed by a guardian, the guardian must (1) provide notice of the hearing to any living parent of the child by personal service at least 30 days before the hearing, or (2) if either or both parents are deceased or cannot be located, serve notice of the hearing on the child's grandparents, if living, not less than 30 days before the hearing under Code of Civil Procedure section 413.10, 414.10, 415.10, or 415.40. *(This Note is included for the information of the petitioner and shall not be included in the Order to Show Cause published in the newspaper.)*

Form Adopted for Mandatory Use
Judicial Council of California
NC-120 [New January 1, 2001]

**ORDER TO SHOW CAUSE
FOR CHANGE OF NAME**
(Change of Name)

WEST GROUP
Official Publisher

Code of Civil Procedure, § 1277

PETITIONER OR ATTORNEY *(Name, state bar number, and address)*:	FOR COURT USE ONLY
TELEPHONE NO.: FAX NO. *(Optional)*: E-MAIL ADDRESS *(Optional)*: ATTORNEY FOR *(Name)*:	

SUPERIOR COURT OF CALIFORNIA, COUNTY OF
STREET ADDRESS:
MAILING ADDRESS:
CITY AND ZIP CODE:
BRANCH NAME:

PETITION OF *(Names of each petitioners)*:

FOR CHANGE OF NAME

DECREE CHANGING NAME	CASE NUMBER:

1. The petition came regularly for hearing on *(date)*:   in Courtroom: of the above-entitled court.

THE COURT FINDS

2. a. All notices required by law have been given.
   b. Each person whose name is to be changed identified in item 3 below
      (1) ☐ is not ☐ is   under the jurisdiction of the Department of Corrections, and
      (2) ☐ is not ☐ is   required to register as a sex offender under section 290 of the Penal Code.
      These determinations were made ☐ by using CLETS/CJIS ☐ based on information provided to the clerk of the court by a local law enforcement agency.
   c. ☐ No objections to the proposed change of name were made.
   d. ☐ Objections to the proposed change of name were made by *(name)*:

   e. It appears to the satisfaction of the court that all the allegations in the petition are true and sufficient and that the petition should be granted.
   f. ☐ Other findings *(if any)*:

THE COURT ORDERS

3. The name of

Present name		New name
a. _____	is changed to	_____
b. _____	is changed to	_____
c. _____	is changed to	_____
d. _____	is changed to	_____
e. _____	is changed to	_____

☐ Additional name changes are listed on Attachment 3.

Date: _____

_____
JUDGE OF THE SUPERIOR COURT
☐ SIGNATURE OF JUDGE FOLLOWS LAST ATTACHMENT

Form Adopted for Mandatory Use
Judicial Council of California
NC-130 [New January 1, 2001]

DECREE CHANGING NAME
(Change of Name)

WEST GROUP
Official Publisher

Code of Civil Procedure, §§ 1278, 1279

ATTORNEY OR PARTY WITHOUT ATTORNEY (Name, state bar number, and address):

FOR COURT USE ONLY

TELEPHONE NO.:   FAX NO.:

ATTORNEY FOR (Name):

INSERT NAME OF COURT, JUDICIAL DISTRICT, AND BRANCH COURT, IF ANY:

CASE NAME:

| **CIVIL CASE COVER SHEET**
 ☐ Limited ☐ Unlimited | **Complex Case Designation**
 ☐ Counter ☐ Joinder
 Filed with first appearance by defendant
 (Cal. Rules of Court, rule 1811) | CASE NUMBER:

 ASSIGNED JUDGE: |

Please complete all five (5) items below.

1. Check **one** box below for the case type that best describes this case:

Auto Tort
☐ Auto (22)

Other PI/PD/WD (Personal Injury/Property Damage/Wrongful Death) Tort
☐ Asbestos (04)
☐ Product liability (24)
☐ Medical malpractice (45)
☐ Other PI/PD/WD (23)

Non-PI/PD/WD (Other) Tort
☐ Business tort/unfair business practice (07)
☐ Civil rights (e.g., discrimination, false arrest) (08)
☐ Defamation (e.g., slander, libel) (13)
☐ Fraud (16)
☐ Intellectual property (19)
☐ Professional negligence (e.g., legal malpractice) (25)
☐ Other non-PI/PD/WD tort (35)

Employment
☐ Wrongful termination (36)

☐ Other employment (15)

Contract
☐ Breach of contract/warranty (06)
☐ Collections (e.g., money owed, open book accounts) (09)
☐ Insurance coverage (18)
☐ Other contract (37)

Real Property
☐ Eminent domain/Inverse condemnation (14)
☐ Wrongful eviction (33)
☐ Other real property (e.g., quiet title) (26)

Unlawful Detainer
☐ Commercial (31)
☐ Residential (32)
☐ Drugs (38)

Judicial Review
☐ Asset forfeiture (05)
☐ Petition re: arbitration award (11)

☐ Writ of mandate (02)
☐ Other judicial review (39)

Provisionally Complex Civil Litigation (Cal. Rules of Court, rules 1800–1812)
☐ Antitrust/Trade regulation (03)
☐ Construction defect (10)
☐ Claims involving mass tort (40)
☐ Securities litigation (28)
☐ Toxic tort/Environmental (30)
☐ Insurance coverage claims arising from the above listed provisionally complex case types (41)

Enforcement of Judgment
☐ Enforcement of judgment (e.g., sister state, foreign, out-of-county abstracts) (20)

Miscellaneous Civil Complaint
☐ RICO (27)
☐ Other complaint (not specified above) (42)

Miscellaneous Civil Petition
☐ Partnership and corporate governance (21)
☒ Other petition (not specified above) (43)

2. This case ☐ is ☒ is not complex under rule 1800 of the California Rules of Court. If case is complex, mark the factors requiring exceptional judicial management:
   a. ☐ Large number of separately represented parties   d. ☐ Large number of witnesses
   b. ☐ Extensive motion practice raising difficult or novel   e. ☐ Coordination and related actions pending in one or more courts issues that will be time-consuming to resolve   in other counties, states or countries, or in a federal court
   c. ☐ Substantial amount of documentary evidence   f. ☐ Substantial post-disposition judicial disposition

3. Type of remedies sought (check all that apply):
   a. ☐ monetary   b. ☒ nonmonetary; declaratory or injunctive relief   c. ☐ punitive

4. Number of causes of action (specify):   one

5. This case ☐ is ☒ is not a class action suit.

Date:

▶

. . . .
(TYPE OR PRINT NAME)   (SIGNATURE OF PARTY OR ATTORNEY FOR PARTY)

NOTICE

- Plaintiff must file this cover sheet with the first paper filed in the action or proceeding (except small claims cases or cases filed under the Probate, Family, or Welfare and Institutions Code). (Cal. Rules of Court, rule 982.2.)
- File this cover sheet in addition to any cover sheet required by local court rule.
- If this case is complex under rule 1800 et seq. of the California Rules of Court, you must serve a copy of this cover sheet on all other parties to the action or proceeding.
- Unless this is a complex case, this cover sheet shall be used for statistical purposes only.

Form Adopted for Mandatory Use
Judicial Council of California
982.2(b)(1) [Rev. January 1, 2000]

CIVIL CASE COVER SHEET

WEST GROUP
Official Publisher

Cal. Rules of Court, rules 982.2, 1800–1812;
Standards of Judicial Administration, § 19

— *THIS FORM MUST BE KEPT CONFIDENTIAL* — 982(a)(17)

ATTORNEY OR PARTY WITHOUT ATTORNEY *(Name, state bar number, and address)*:	FOR COURT USE ONLY

TELEPHONE NO.:   FAX NO. *(Optional)*:

E-MAIL ADDRESS *(Optional)*:

ATTORNEY FOR *(Name)*:

NAME OF COURT:

STREET ADDRESS:

MAILING ADDRESS:

CITY AND ZIP CODE:

BRANCH NAME:

PLAINTIFF/ PETITIONER:

DEFENDANT/ RESPONDENT:

**APPLICATION FOR
WAIVER OF COURT FEES AND COSTS**

CASE NUMBER:

I request a court order so that I do not have to pay court fees and costs.

1. a. ☐ I am **not** able to pay any of the court fees and costs.
   b. ☐ I am able to pay **only** the following court fees and costs *(specify)*:

2. My current street or mailing address is *(if applicable, include city or town, apartment no., if any, and zip code)*:

3. a. My occupation, employer, and employer's address are *(specify)*:

   b. My spouse's occupation, employer, and employer's address are *(specify)*:

4. ☐ I am receiving financial assistance under one or more of the following programs:
   a. ☐ **SSI and SSP:** Supplemental Security Income and State Supplemental Payments Programs
   b. ☐ **CalWORKs:** California Work Opportunity and Responsibility to Kids Act, implementing TANF, Temporary Assistance for Needy Families (formerly AFDC)
   c. ☐ **Food Stamps:** The Food Stamp Program
   d. ☐ **County Relief, General Relief (G.R.), or General Assistance (G.A.)**

5. If you checked box 4, you must check and complete **one of the three boxes below, unless you are a defendant in an unlawful detainer action. Do not check more than one box.**
   a. ☐ *(Optional)* My Medi-Cal number is *(specify)*:
   b. ☐ *(Optional)* My social security number is *(specify)*:
      ☐☐☐ – ☐☐ – ☐☐☐☐ and my date of birth is *(specify)*:
      [Federal law does not require that you give your social security number. However, if you don't give your social security number, you must check box c and attach documents to verify the benefits checked in item 4.]
   c. ☐ I am attaching documents to verify receipt of the benefits checked in item 4, if requested by the court.
      [See Form 982(a)(17)(A) Information Sheet on Waiver of Court Fees and Costs, available from the clerk's office, for a list of acceptable documents.]

[If you checked box 4 above, skip items 6 and 7, and sign at the bottom of this side.]

6. ☐ My total gross monthly household income is less than the amount shown on the *Information Sheet on Waiver of Court Fees and Costs* available from the clerk's office.

[If you checked box 6 above, skip item 7, complete items 8, 9a, 9d, 9f, and 9g on the back of this form, and sign at the bottom of this side.]

7. ☐ My income is not enough to pay for the common necessaries of life for me and the people in my family whom I support and also pay court fees and costs. *[If you check this box, you must complete the back of this form.]*

WARNING: You must immediately tell the court if you become able to pay court fees or costs during this action. You may be ordered to appear in court and answer questions about your ability to pay court fees or costs.

I declare under penalty of perjury under the laws of the State of California that the information on both sides of this form and all attachments are true and correct.

Date:

▶

_____ _____
(TYPE OR PRINT NAME)   (Financial information on reverse)   (SIGNATURE)

Form Adopted for Mandatory Use
Judicial Council of California
982(a)(17) [Rev. January 1, 2001]

**APPLICATION FOR WAIVER OF COURT FEES AND COSTS
(In Forma Pauperis)**

WEST GROUP
Official Publisher

Government Code,
§ 68511.3

PLAINTIFF/PETITIONER:	CASE NUMBER:
DEFENDANT/RESPONDENT:	

FINANCIAL INFORMATION

8. ☐ My pay changes considerably from month to month. *[If you check this box, each of the amounts reported in item 9 should be your average for the past 12 months.]*

9. **MY MONTHLY INCOME**

a. My gross monthly pay is: . . . . $ _____

b. **My payroll deductions are (specify purpose and amount):**

(1) _____	$ _____
(2) _____	$ _____
(3) _____	$ _____
(4) _____	$ _____

My TOTAL payroll deduction amount is: $ _____

c. My monthly take-home pay is
(a. minus b.): . . . . $ _____

d. Other money I get each month is *(specify **source** and **amount**; include spousal support, child support, parental support, support from outside the home, scholarships, retirement or pensions, social security, disability, unemployment, military basic allowance for quarters (BAQ), veterans payments, dividends, interest or royalty, trust income, annuities, net business income, net rental income, reimbursement of job-related expenses, and net gambling or lottery winnings):*

(1) _____	$ _____
(2) _____	$ _____
(3) _____	$ _____
(4) _____	$ _____

The TOTAL amount of other money is: $ _____
(If more space is needed, attach page labeled Attachment 9d.)

e. **MY TOTAL MONTHLY INCOME IS**
(c. plus d.): . . . . $ _____

f. Number of persons living in my home: _____
Below list all the persons living in your home, including your spouse, who depend in whole or in part on you for support, **or** on whom you depend in whole or in part for support:

	Name	Age	Relationship	Gross Monthly Income
(1)	_____	____	_____	$ _____
(2)	_____	____	_____	$ _____
(3)	_____	____	_____	$ _____
(4)	_____	____	_____	$ _____
(5)	_____	____	_____	$ _____

The TOTAL amount of other money is: $ _____
(If more space is needed, attach page labeled Attachment 9f.)

g. **MY TOTAL GROSS MONTHLY HOUSEHOLD INCOME IS**
(a. plus d. plus f.): . . . . $ _____

10. **I own or have an interest in the following property:**

a. Cash . . . . $ _____

b. Checking, savings, and credit union accounts *(list banks):*

(1) _____	$ _____
(2) _____	$ _____
(3) _____	$ _____
(4) _____	$ _____

c. Cars, other vehicles, and boats *(list make, year, fair market value (FMV), and loan balance of each):*

	Property	FMV	Loan Balance
(1)	_____	$ _____	$ _____
(2)	_____	$ _____	$ _____
(3)	_____	$ _____	$ _____

d. Real estate *(list address, estimated fair market value (FMV), and loan balance of each property):*

	Property	FMV	Loan Balance
(1)	_____	$ _____	$ _____
(2)	_____	$ _____	$ _____
(3)	_____	$ _____	$ _____

e. Other personal property — jewelry, furniture, furs, stocks, bonds, etc. *(list separately):*

$ _____

11. **My monthly expenses not already listed in item 9b above are the following:**

a. Rent or house payment & maintenance $ _____
b. Food and household supplies . . . . $ _____
c. Utilities and telephone . . . . $ _____
d. Clothing . . . . $ _____
e. Laundry and cleaning . . . . $ _____
f. Medical and dental payments . . . . $ _____
g. Insurance (life, health, accident, etc.) . . $ _____
h. School, child care . . . . $ _____
i. Child, spousal support (prior marriage) . . $ _____
j. Transportation and auto expenses
(insurance, gas, repair) . . . . $ _____
k. Installment payments *(specify **purpose** and **amount**):*

(1) _____	$ _____
(2) _____	$ _____
(3) _____	$ _____

The TOTAL amount of monthly installment payments is: . . . . $ _____

l. Amounts deducted due to wage assignments and earnings withholding orders: $ _____

m. Other expenses *(specify):*

(1) _____	$ _____
(2) _____	$ _____
(3) _____	$ _____
(4) _____	$ _____
(5) _____	$ _____

The TOTAL amount of other monthly expenses is: . . . . $ _____

n. **MY TOTAL MONTHLY EXPENSES ARE**
(add a. through m.): . . . . $ _____

12. Other facts that support this application are *(describe unusual medical needs, expenses for recent family emergencies, or other unusual circumstances or expenses to help the court understand your budget; if more space is needed, attach page labeled Attachment 12):*

WARNING: You must immediately tell the court if you become able to pay court fees or costs during this action. You may be ordered to appear in court and answer questions about your ability to pay court fees or costs.

ATTORNEY OR PARTY WITHOUT ATTORNEY *(Name, state bar number, and address):*	FOR COURT USE ONLY

TELEPHONE NO.:   FAX NO.:

ATTORNEY FOR *(Name):*

NAME OF COURT:

STREET ADDRESS:

MAILING ADDRESS:

CITY AND ZIP CODE:

BRANCH NAME:

PLAINTIFF/ PETITIONER:

DEFENDANT/ RESPONDENT:

ORDER ON APPLICATION FOR WAIVER OF COURT FEES AND COSTS	CASE NUMBER:

1. The application was filed on *(date):* ☐ A previous order was issued on *(date):*
2. The application was filed by *(name):*
3. ☐ IT IS ORDERED that the application is **granted** ☐ in whole ☐ in part *(see Cal. Rules of Court, rule 985).*
   - a. ☐ **No payments.** Payment of all the fees and costs listed in California Rules of Court, rule 985(i), **is waived.**
   - b. ☐ **The applicant shall pay** all the fees and costs listed in California Rules of Court, rule 985(i), EXCEPT the following:
     - (1) ☐ Filing papers.
     - (2) ☐ Certification and copying.
     - (3) ☐ Issuing process and certification.
     - (4) ☐ Transmittal of papers.
     - (5) ☐ Court-appointed interpreter *(small claims only).*
     - (6) ☐ Sheriff and marshal fees.
     - (7) ☐ Reporter's fees* *(valid for 60 days).*
     - (8) ☐ Telephone appearance (Gov. Code, § 68070.1(c))
     - (9) ☐ Other *(specify code section):*

     * Reporter's fees are per diem pursuant to Code Civ. Proc., §§ 269, 274c, and Gov. Code, §§ 69947, 69948, and 72195.
   - c. **Method of payment.** The applicant shall pay all the fees and costs when charged, EXCEPT as follows:
     - (1) ☐ Pay *(specify):* percent. (2) ☐ Pay: $ per month or more until the balance is paid.
   - d. The clerk of the court, county financial officer, or appropriate county officer is authorized to require the litigant to appear before and be examined by the court no sooner than four months from the date of this order, and not more than once in any four-month period. ☐ The applicant is ordered to appear in this court as follows for review of his or her financial status:

Date:	Time:	Dept.:	Div.:	Room:

   - e. ☐ *(must be completed if application is granted in part)* Reasons for denial of a requested waiver *(specify):*

   - f. ☐ The clerk is directed to mail a copy of this order to the applicant's attorney or to the applicant if unrepresented.
   - g. **All unpaid fees and costs shall be deemed to be taxable costs if the applicant is entitled to costs and shall be a lien on any judgment recovered by the applicant and shall be paid directly to the clerk by the judgment debtor upon such recovery.**
4. ☐ IT IS ORDERED that the application is **denied** for the following reasons *(specify):*

   - a. The applicant shall pay any fees and costs due in this action within 10 days from the date of service of this order or any paper filed by the applicant with the clerk will be of no effect.
   - b. The clerk is directed to mail a copy of this order to all parties who have appeared in this action.
5. ☐ IT IS ORDERED that a **hearing** be held.
   - a. The substantial evidentiary conflict to be resolved by the hearing is *(specify):*

   - b. The applicant should appear in this court at the following hearing to help resolve the conflict:

Date:	Time:	Dept.:	Div.:	Room:

   - c. The address of the court is *(specify):*
   - d. The clerk is directed to mail a copy of this order to the applicant only.

NOTICE: If item 3d or item 5b is filled in and the applicant does not attend the hearing, the court may revoke or change the order or deny the application without considering information the applicant wants the court to consider.

WARNING: The applicant must immediately tell the court if he or she becomes able to pay court fees or costs during this action. The applicant may be ordered to appear in court and answer questions about his or her ability to pay fees or costs.

Date: _____

_____
(Continued on reverse) JUDICIAL OFFICER

Form Adopted by Rule 982
Judicial Council of California
982(a)(18) [Rev. January 1, 1999]

ORDER ON APPLICATION FOR WAIVER OF COURT FEES AND COSTS (In Forma Pauperis)

WEST GROUP
Official Publisher

Government Code, § 68511.3; Cal. Rules of Court, rule 985

PLAINTIFF/PETITIONER (Name):	CASE NUMBER:
DEFENDANT/RESPONDENT (Name):	

CLERK'S CERTIFICATE OF MAILING

I certify that I am not a party to this cause and that a true copy of the foregoing was mailed first class, postage prepaid, in a sealed envelope addressed as shown below, and that the mailing of the foregoing and execution of this certificate occurred at
(place):   , California,
on (date):

Clerk, by _____ , Deputy

(SEAL)

CLERK'S CERTIFICATE

I certify that the foregoing is a true and correct copy of the original on file in my office.

Date: Clerk, by _____ , Deputy

PETITION OF (Name of petitioner or petitioners): FOR CHANGE OF NAME	CASE NUMBER:

DECLARATION OF GUARDIAN
Supplemental Attachment to *Petition for Change of Name* (Form NC-100)   **Attachment** _____ **of** _____
*(If you are petitioning as a guardian of a minor, you must use a **separate** supplemental attachment for **each minor** whose name is to be changed.)*

7. a. Petitioner (name):

    b. Petitioner's address (street, city, county, and zip code):

    c. Petitioner is the guardian of the following minor whose name is to be changed:
       (1) Name (present name of child):
       (2) Address (street, city, county, and zip code):

    d. Petitioner was appointed guardian of the minor identified in item 7c by (specify):
       (1) Superior Court of California, County of (name):
       (2) Department (check one): ☐ Juvenile   ☐ Probate
       (3) Case number (specify):
       (4) Date of appointment (specify):

    e. The grandparents of the minor whose name is to be changed are (provide names and addresses, if known):
       (1) Grandfather (name):   (address):

       (2) Grandmother (name):   (address):

       (3) Grandfather (name):   (address):

       (4) Grandmother (name):   (address):

    f. The minor identified in item 7c is likely to remain under the guardian's care until the minor reaches the age of majority because (explain):

       ☐ Continued (if you need additional space, check the box, prepare an Attachment 7f, and attach it to this declaration).
    g. The minor identified in item 7c is not likely to be returned to the custody of his or her parents because (explain):

       ☐ Continued (if you need additional space, check the box, prepare an Attachment 7g, and attach it to this declaration).
    h. Other relevant information about the guardianship and why the proposed name change is in the best interest of the minor (specify):

       ☐ Continued (if you need additional space, check the box, prepare an Attachment 7h, and attach it to this declaration).

I declare under penalty of perjury under the laws of the State of California that the information in the foregoing declaration is true and correct.

Date:

▶

_____   _____
(TYPE OR PRINT NAME)   (SIGNATURE OF PETITIONER)

Guardian of (name of minor):

Form Adopted for Mandatory Use
Judicial Council of California
NC-110G [New January 1, 2001]

SUPPLEMENTAL ATTACHMENT TO
PETITION FOR CHANGE OF NAME
(Declaration of Guardian)

WEST GROUP
Official Publisher

Code of Civil Procedure, § 1275 et seq.

PETITIONER OR ATTORNEY *(Name, state bar number, and address)*:	FOR COURT USE ONLY

TELEPHONE NO.:   FAX NO. *(Optional)*:

E-MAIL ADDRESS *(Optional)*:

ATTORNEY FOR *(Name)*:

SUPERIOR COURT OF CALIFORNIA, COUNTY OF

STREET ADDRESS:

MAILING ADDRESS:

CITY AND ZIP CODE:

BRANCH NAME:

PETITION OF *(Names of each petitioner)*:

FOR CHANGE OF NAME

DECREE CHANGING NAME OF MINOR (BY GUARDIAN)	CASE NUMBER:

1. The petition came regularly for hearing on *(date)*:   in Courtroom: of the above-entitled court.

THE COURT FINDS

2. a. All notices required by law have been given.

   b. The person whose name is to be changed *(specify present name)*:
      is a minor.

   c. The petition for change of name was filed on behalf of the minor by the minor's guardian *(name)*:

   d. The minor whose name is to be changed is likely to remain in the guardian's care until the age of majority.

   e. The minor whose name is to be changed is not likely to be returned to the custody of his or her parents.

   f. The minor whose name is to be changed

     (1) ☐ is not ☐ is   under the jurisdiction of the Department of Corrections, and

     (2) ☐ is not ☐ is   required to register as a sex offender under section 290 of the Penal Code.

     These determinations were made ☐ by using CLETS/CJIS ☐ based on information provided to the clerk of the court by a local law enforcement agency.

   g. ☐ No objections to the proposed change of name were made.

   h. ☐ Objections to the proposed change of name were made by *(name)*:

   i. It appears to the satisfaction of the court that all the allegations in the petition are true and sufficient, that the proposed name change is in the best interest of the minor, and that the petition should be granted.

   j. ☐ Other findings *(if any)*:

THE COURT ORDERS

3. The name of *(present name)*:
   is changed to *(new name)*:

Date:

                                    JUDGE OF THE SUPERIOR COURT

                       ☐ SIGNATURE OF JUDGE FOLLOWS LAST ATTACHMENT

Form Adopted for Mandatory Use
Judicial Council of California
NC-130G [New January 1, 2001]

DECREE CHANGING NAME
(Change of Name of Minor by Guardian)

WEST GROUP
Official Publisher

Code of Civil Procedure, §§ 1278, 1279

PETITIONER OR ATTORNEY (Name, state bar number, and address):	FOR COURT USE ONLY
TELEPHONE NO.: FAX NO. (Optional):	
E-MAIL ADDRESS (Optional):	
ATTORNEY FOR (Name):	

SUPERIOR COURT OF CALIFORNIA, COUNTY OF STREET ADDRESS: MAILING ADDRESS: CITY AND ZIP CODE: BRANCH NAME:	
PETITION OF (Names of each petitioner): FOR CHANGE OF NAME	
PROOF OF SERVICE OF ORDER TO SHOW CAUSE BY ☐ PERSONAL DELIVERY ☐ MAILING (OUTSIDE CALIFORNIA ONLY)	CASE NUMBER:

1. At the time of mailing or personal delivery, I was at least 18 years of age and **not a party** to this proceeding.

2. My residence or business address is (specify):

3. I personally delivered or mailed a copy of the *Order to Show Cause for Change of Name* as follows (complete either a or b):

   a. ☐ **Personal delivery.** I personally delivered a copy to the person served as follows:

      (1) Name of person served:

      (2) Address where delivered:

      (3) Date delivered:

      (4) Time delivered:

   b. ☐ **Mail.** I am a resident of or employed in the county where the mailing occurred.

      (1) I enclosed a copy in an envelope and mailed the sealed envelope to the person served by first-class mail, postage prepaid, return receipt requested, to the address outside of California listed below.

      (2) The envelope was addressed and mailed as follows:

         (a) Name of person served:

         (b) Address on envelope:

         (c) Date of mailing:

         (d) Place of mailing (city and state):

I declare under penalty of perjury under the laws of the State of California that the foregoing is true and correct.

Date:

▶

_____
(TYPE OR PRINT NAME OF DECLARANT)

_____
(SIGNATURE OF DECLARANT)

Form Adopted for Mandatory Use
Judicial Council of California
NC-121 [New January 1, 2001]

**PROOF OF SERVICE OF
ORDER TO SHOW CAUSE**
(Change of Name)

WEST GROUP
Official Publisher

Code of Civil Procedure, § 1277

1
2
3
4
5
6
7
8
9
10
11
12
13
14
15
16
17
18
19
20
21
22
23
24
25
26
27
28

DECLARATION RESTORING FORMER LEGAL NAME

I, the undersigned, declare that I am 18 years of age or older and further declare:

1. The name I am presently using is _____.

2. My marital status is as follows *(optional):*

    a. ❑ I was legally divorced in the State of _____ on

    _____.

    b. ❑ My marriage was legally annulled in the State of _____ on

    _____.

    c. ❑ I am legally married.

    d. ❑ I am single.

3. I HEREBY DECLARE my intent to return to my former legal name, and be henceforth exclusively known

as _____.

4. I have no intention of defrauding any person or escaping any obligation I may presently have by this act.

5. NOTICE IS HEREBY GIVEN to all agencies of the State of California, all agencies of the Federal Government, all creditors and all private persons, groups, businesses, corporations and associations of said legal name change.

I declare under penalty of perjury under the laws of the State of California that the foregoing is true and correct.

Dated: _____   _____
                                        (new signature)

                                        _____
                                        (old signature)

NOTARIZATION

State of California

County of _____ } ss

On this _____ day of _____, _____ , before me, _____,
a notary public of the State of California, personally appeared _____,
personally known to me (or proved to me on the basis of satisfactory evidence) to be the person(s) whose
name(s) is/are subscribed to the within instrument, and acknowledged to me that she/he/they executed the same
in her/his/their authorized capacity(ies), and that by her/his/their signature(s) on the instrument the person(s), or
the entity upon behalf of which the person(s) acted, executed the instrument.

WITNESS my hand and official seal. _____
                                        Signature of Notary Public

[Notary Seal]   Notary Public for the State of California

                                        My commission expires: _____, _____

DECLARATION OF LEGAL NAME CHANGE

I, the undersigned, declare that I am 18 years of age or older and further declare:

1. I, _____, was born _____ in

_____ County in the State of _____ on _____.

2. I HEREBY DECLARE my intent to change my legal name, and be henceforth exclusively known as

_____.

3. I further declare that I have no intention of defrauding any person or escaping any obligation I may presently have by this act.

4. NOTICE IS HEREBY GIVEN to all agencies of the State of California, all agencies of the Federal Government, all creditors and all private persons, groups, businesses, corporations and associations of said legal name change.

I declare under penalty of perjury under the laws of the State of California that the foregoing is true and correct.

Dated: _____   _____
                                                                      (new signature)

                                                _____
                                                                      (old signature)

NOTARIZATION

State of California

County of _____ } ss

On this _____ day of _____, _____, before me, _____

_____, a notary public of the State of California, personally

appeared _____, personally known to me (or proved

to me on the basis of satisfactory evidence) to be the person(s) whose name(s) is/are subscribed to the within instrument, and acknowledged to me that she/he/they executed the same in her/his/their authorized capacities, and that by her/his/their signature(s) on the instrument the person(s), or the entity upon behalf of which the person(s) acted, executed the instrument.

WITNESS my hand and official seal. _____
                                                                    Signature of Notary Public

[Notary Seal]   Notary Public for the State of California

                                                My commission expires: _____, _____

Changing Your Name by the Usage Method

In California, adults can legally change their names in two ways, either by filing a court petition or by consistently using their new name for all business purposes without going to court. California's legislature and courts have long recognized the right of adults to change their names without petitioning a court. For example, the most respected legal treatise relied on by judges, lawyers and law students, *Summary of California Law* (Witkin), states, "A person has a common law right to change his name without applying to a court." Witkin, 4 Summary of Cal. L., Ch. VIII, § 16 (9th Ed. 1987).

True, the California legislature has also created a process by which a person may go to court to change his name. Described in Civil Procedure Code Sections 1275 to 1279.6, this process is designed to record a person's change. None of these laws alter the fact that California courts have repeatedly stated that changing your name by consistently using a new name is legal:

"A person may change his name any time without initiating legal proceedings." *In re Marriage of Banks*, 42 Cal. App. 3d 631 (1974).

"The common law recognizes a right of a person to change his name without the necessity of legal proceedings; the purpose of the statutory procedure is simply to have, wherever possible, the change recorded." *In re Ritchie*, 159 Cal. App. 3d 1070 (1984).

An adult "has a common law right to change his name…without the necessity of any legal proceeding." *Lee v. Ventura County Superior Court*, 9 Cal. App. 4th 510 (1992).

Since Californians clearly have the legal right to change their names by consistently using a new name in place of an old one, private businesses and governmental agencies should be willing to change all records reflecting a person's name upon request.

Index

DMV (Department of Motor Vehicles)
gender/name changes by, 6/21
name change regulations at, 1/2-3, 4/3,
4/5, 7/3
new driver's license from, 7/3, 7/6
Domestic violence, victims of, 6/9, 6/14, 6/15
Driver's license, 1/2-3, 4/3, 4/5, 7/3, 7/6
Due Diligence Declaration
sample form, 6/30
with waiver of notification, 6/32
when to use, 6/29

E

Ex Parte Application for Restoration of
Former Name After Entry of Judgment and
Order, 6/2
blank form, Appendix
completing the form, 4/5
sample form, 4/6

F

Famous names, 3/2-3
Fees
Application for Waiver of, 6/15-18
of attorneys, 1/4, 8/4-5
to file Petition, 1/3-4
for publication of Order to Show Cause,
6/25
Fictitious names, 3/3
FindLaw website, 8/7
First names
methods to change, 2/4-5
use of multiple, 2/2, 2/4

Former name
court-ordered restoration of, 1/4, 4/5, 6/2
restored after divorce, 4/5
restored during divorce, 4/4
restored during marriage, 4/3-4
Usage method to restore, 7/2-3
Forms of address as names, 3/5

G

Gender information
on adult's new birth certificate, 5/6, 5/7
on child's new birth certificate, 5/4
corrected by DMV, 6/21
corrected on name change forms, 6/21-22
Government agency notification of name
change, 7/3, 7/6, 7/8-14

H

Health Services Department website, 5/7

I

ID cards, 1/2-3, 4/3, 4/5, 7/3, 7/6
Identity theft, 1/2-3
Immigrant names, Introduction/2
Information Sheet on Waiver of Court Fees
and Costs (California Judicial Council), 6/16
Initials
as names, 3/3
with one-word name, 3/4

W

■

Document Preparation Services

The following is a paid listing of paralegal offices that offer document preparation services in California.

81 Legal Doc Service
Joyce Chan
P.O. Box 1632
BURLINGAME, CA 94011
mobile phone: 415-350-1263
email: jlc81@ix.netcom.com
Year established: 1995
LDA#: 04

Fremont Divorce and Document Services
Marcia Burke
39159 Paseo Padre Parkway #110
FREMONT, CA 94538
phone: 510-791-2700
fax: 510-791-2798
email: d7rlegal@aol.com
Year established: 1980
LDA#: 02

Lynne Stein Legal Document Assistance
Lynne Stein/Margaret Fazio
1430 Second St.
LIVERMORE, CA 94550
phone: 925-373-0444
fax: 925-373-0453
email: stein53@aol.com
Year established: 1987
LDA#: 004/005

EZ Law Paralegal Services
Amora Johnson
12702 Magnolia Ave. #23
RIVERSIDE, CA 92503
phone: 909-279-5277
fax: 909-279-5249
Year established: 1990
LDA#: 0049

Gerald (Budd) Westreich
2355 El Camino Ave #A
SACRAMENTO, CA 95821
phone: 916-483-0306
fax: 916-483-0328
email: gwestre194@aol.com
Year established: 1992
LDA#: 2001-01

People's Legal Services
Kerry Suendermann
1380 Lincoln Ave. Ste. 4
SAN RAFAEL, CA 94901
phone: 415-453-5952
fax: 415-453-4190
email: ldalegal@home.com
website: peopleslegalservices.com
Year established: 1982
LDA#: 21/002

Delta Typing Service
Barbara Jantzen
3232 N. El Dorado St.
STOCKTON, CA 95204
phone: 209-948-2583
fax: 209-948-4762
email: deltatyping@hotmail.com
Year established: 1978
LDA#: 02

LDA#: Paralegals who serve the public are called LDAs (Legal Documents Assistants) and must register in their counties. The LDA# shown is for the county where the office is located.

Offices have been listed in alphabetical order by city.

Paid Advertising

CATALOG

...more from Nolo

	PRICE	CODE
BUSINESS		
Avoid Employee Lawsuits (Quick & Legal Series)	$24.95	AVEL
The CA Nonprofit Corporation Kit (Binder w/CD-ROM)	$59.95	CNP
Consultant & Independent Contractor Agreements (Book w/CD-ROM)	$29.95	CICA
The Corporate Minutes Book (Book w/CD-ROM)	$69.95	CORMI
The Employer's Legal Handbook	$39.95	EMPL
Firing Without Fear (Quick & Legal Series)	$29.95	FEAR
Form Your Own Limited Liability Company (Book w/CD-ROM)	$44.95	LIAB
Hiring Independent Contractors: The Employer's Legal Guide (Book w/CD-ROM)	$34.95	HICI
How to Create a Buy-Sell Agreement & Control the Destiny of your Small Business (Book w/Disk-PC)	$49.95	BSAG
How to Form a California Professional Corporation (Book w/CD-ROM)	$59.95	PROF
How to Form a Nonprofit Corporation (Book w/CD-ROM)—National Edition	$44.95	NNP
How to Form a Nonprofit Corporation in California (Book w/CD-ROM)	$44.95	NON
How to Form Your Own California Corporation (Binder w/CD-ROM)	$39.95	CACI
How to Form Your Own California Corporation (Book w/CD-ROM)	$34.95	CCOR
How to Form Your Own New York Corporation (Book w/Disk—PC)	$39.95	NYCO
How to Form Your Own Texas Corporation (Book w/CD-ROM)	$39.95	TCOR
How to Write a Business Plan	$29.95	SBS
The Independent Paralegal's Handbook	$29.95	PARA
Leasing Space for Your Small Business	$34.95	LESP
Legal Guide for Starting & Running a Small Business	$34.95	RUNS
Legal Forms for Starting & Running a Small Business (Book w/CD-ROM)	$29.95	RUNS2
Marketing Without Advertising	$22.00	MWAD
Music Law (Book w/Disk—PC)	$29.95	ML
Nolo's California Quick Corp (Quick & Legal Series)	$19.95	QINC
Nolo's Guide to Social Security Disability	$29.95	QSS
Nolo's Quick LLC (Quick & Legal Series)	$24.95	LLCQ
The Small Business Start-up Kit (Book w/CD-ROM)	$29.95	SMBU
The Small Business Start-up Kit for California (Book w/CD-ROM)	$29.95	OPEN
The Partnership Book: How to Write a Partnership Agreement (Book w/CD-ROM)	$39.95	PART
Sexual Harassment on the Job	$24.95	HARS

	PRICE	CODE
Starting & Running a Successful Newsletter or Magazine	$29.95	MAG
Tax Savvy for Small Business	$34.95	SAVVY
Working for Yourself: Law & Taxes for the Self-Employed	$39.95	WAGE
Your Limited Liability Company: An Operating Manual (Book w/Disk—PC)	$49.95	LOP
Your Rights in the Workplace	$29.95	YRW

CONSUMER

	PRICE	CODE
Fed Up with the Legal System: What's Wrong & How to Fix It	$9.95	LEG
How to Win Your Personal Injury Claim	$29.95	PICL
Nolo's Encyclopedia of Everyday Law	$28.95	EVL
Nolo's Pocket Guide to California Law	$15.95	CLAW
Trouble-Free Travel...And What to Do When Things Go Wrong	$14.95	TRAV

ESTATE PLANNING & PROBATE

	PRICE	CODE
8 Ways to Avoid Probate (Quick & Legal Series)	$16.95	PRO8
9 Ways to Avoid Estate Taxes (Quick & Legal Series)	$29.95	ESTX
Estate Planning Basics (Quick & Legal Series)	$18.95	ESPN
How to Probate an Estate in California	$49.95	PAE
Make Your Own Living Trust (Book w/CD-ROM)	$34.95	LITR
Nolo's Law Form Kit: Wills	$24.95	KWL
Nolo's Simple Will Book (Book w/CD-ROM)	$34.95	SWIL
Plan Your Estate	$39.95	NEST
Quick & Legal Will Book (Quick & Legal Series)	$15.95	QUIC

FAMILY MATTERS

	PRICE	CODE
Child Custody: Building Parenting Agreements That Work	$29.95	CUST
The Complete IEP Guide	$24.95	IEP
Divorce & Money: How to Make the Best Financial Decisions During Divorce	$34.95	DIMO
Do Your Own Divorce in Oregon	$29.95	ODIV
Get a Life: You Don't Need a Million to Retire Well	$24.95	LIFE
The Guardianship Book for California	$34.95	GB
How to Adopt Your Stepchild in California (Book w/CD-ROM)	$34.95	ADOP
A Legal Guide for Lesbian and Gay Couples	$25.95	LG
Living Together: A Legal Guide (Book w/CD-ROM)	$34.95	LTK
Using Divorce Mediation: Save Your Money & Your Sanity	$29.95	UDMD

	PRICE	CODE

IMMIGRATION

How to Get a Green Card	$29.95	GRN
U.S. Immigration Made Easy	$44.95	IMEZ

MONEY MATTERS

101 Law Forms for Personal Use (Book w/Disk—PC)	$29.95	SPOT
Bankruptcy: Is It the Right Solution to Your Debt Problems? (Quick & Legal Series)	$19.95	BRS
Chapter 13 Bankruptcy: Repay Your Debts	$34.95	CH13
Creating Your Own Retirement Plan	$29.95	YROP
Credit Repair (Quick & Legal Series, Book w/CD-ROM)	$19.95	CREP
How to File for Chapter 7 Bankruptcy	$34.95	HFB
IRAs, 401(k)s & Other Retirement Plans: Taking Your Money Out	$29.95	RET
Money Troubles: Legal Strategies to Cope With Your Debts	$29.95	MT
Nolo's Law Form Kit: Personal Bankruptcy	$24.95	KBNK
Stand Up to the IRS	$24.95	SIRS
Surviving an IRS Tax Audit (Quick & Legal Series)	$24.95	SAUD
Take Control of Your Student Loan Debt	$24.95	SLOAN

PATENTS AND COPYRIGHTS

The Copyright Handbook: How to Protect and Use Written Works (Book w/CD-ROM)	$34.95	COHA
Copyright Your Software	$24.95	CYS
Domain Names	$24.95	DOM
Getting Permission: How to License and Clear Copyrighted Materials Online and Off (Book w/Disk—PC)	$34.95	RIPER
How to Make Patent Drawings Yourself	$29.95	DRAW
The Inventor's Notebook	$24.95	INOT
Nolo's Patents for Beginners (Quick & Legal Series)	$29.95	QPAT
License Your Invention (Book w/Disk—PC)	$39.95	LICE
Patent, Copyright & Trademark	$34.95	PCTM
Patent It Yourself	$49.95	PAT
Patent Searching Made Easy	$29.95	PATSE
The Public Domain	$34.95	PUBL
Web and Software Development: A Legal Guide (Book w/ CD-ROM)	$44.95	SFT
Trademark: Legal Care for Your Business and Product Name	$39.95	TRD

RESEARCH & REFERENCE

Legal Research: How to Find & Understand the Law	$34.95	LRES

Order Form

Name

Address

City

State, Zip

Daytime Phone

E-mail

Our "No-Hassle" Guarantee

Return anything you buy directly from Nolo for any reason and we'll cheerfully refund your purchase price. No ifs, ands or buts.

☐ Check here if you do not wish to receive mailings from other companies

Item Code	Quantity	Item	Unit Price	Total Price

Subtotal	
Add your local sales tax (California only)	
Shipping: RUSH $9, Basic $5 (See below)	
"I bought 3, ship it to me FREE!"(Ground shipping only)	
TOTAL	

Method of payment

☐ Check   ☐ VISA   ☐ MasterCard
☐ Discover Card   ☐ American Express

Account Number

Expiration Date

Signature

Shipping and Handling

Rush Delivery—Only $9

We'll ship any order to any street address in the U.S. by UPS 2nd Day Air* for only $9!

* Order by noon Pacific Time and get your order in 2 business days. Orders placed after noon Pacific Time will arrive in 3 business days. P.O. boxes and S.F. Bay Area use basic shipping. Alaska and Hawaii use 2nd Day Air or Priority Mail.

Basic Shipping—$5

Use for P.O. Boxes, Northern California and Ground Service.

Allow 1-2 weeks for delivery. U.S. addresses only.

For faster service, use your credit card and our toll-free numbers

**Call our customer service group
Monday thru Friday 7am to 7pm PST**

Phone	1-800-728-3555
Fax	1-800-645-0895
Mail	Nolo
950 Parker St.
Berkeley, CA 94710

**Order 24 hours a day @
www.nolo.com**

Take 2 Minutes
& Give Us Your 2 cents

Your comments make a big difference in the development and revision of Nolo books and software. Please take a few minutes and register your Nolo product—and your comments—with us. Not only will your input make a difference, you'll receive special offers available only to registered owners of Nolo products on our newest books and software. Register now by:

PHONE
1-800-728-3555

FAX
1-800-645-0895

EMAIL
cs@nolo.com

or **MAIL** us
this registration card

REMEMBER:
Little publishers have big ears. We really listen to you.

fold here

REGISTRATION CARD

NAME	DATE

ADDRESS

CITY	STATE	ZIP
PHONE	E-MAIL	

WHERE DID YOU HEAR ABOUT THIS PRODUCT?

WHERE DID YOU PURCHASE THIS PRODUCT?

DID YOU CONSULT A LAWYER? (PLEASE CIRCLE ONE)   YES   NO   NOT APPLICABLE

DID YOU FIND THIS BOOK HELPFUL?   (VERY)   5   4   3   2   1   (NOT AT ALL)

COMMENTS

WAS IT EASY TO USE?   (VERY EASY)   5   4   3   2   1   (VERY DIFFICULT)

DO YOU OWN A COMPUTER? IF SO, WHICH FORMAT? (PLEASE CIRCLE ONE)   WINDOWS   DOS   MAC

We occasionally make our mailing list available to carefully selected companies whose products may be of interest to you.
❏ If you do not wish to receive mailings from these companies, please check this box.
❏ You can quote me in future Nolo promotional materials. Daytime phone number _____.

NAME 9.0

NOLO IN THE NEWS

"Nolo helps lay people perform legal tasks without the aid—or fees—of lawyers."

—USA TODAY

Nolo books are ..."written in plain language, free of legal mumbo jumbo, and spiced with witty personal observations."

—ASSOCIATED PRESS

"...Nolo publications...guide people simply through the how, when, where and why of law."

—WASHINGTON POST

"Increasingly, people who are not lawyers are performing tasks usually regarded as legal work... And consumers, using books like Nolo's, do routine legal work themselves."

—NEW YORK TIMES

"...All of [Nolo's] books are easy-to-understand, are updated regularly, provide pull-out forms...and are often quite moving in their sense of compassion for the struggles of the lay reader."

—SAN FRANCISCO CHRONICLE

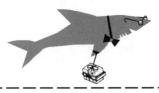

fold here

- -

nolo
950 Parker Street
Berkeley, CA 94710-9867

Attn: | **NAME 9.0** |